EDUCATING FOR INSURGENCY:

The Roles of Young People in Schools of Poverty

EDUCATING FOR INSURGENCY:

The Roles of Young People in Schools of Poverty

Jay Gillen

AK PRESS
EDINBURGH · OAKLAND · BALTIMORE

Educating for Insurgency: The Roles of Young People in Schools of Poverty © 2014 Jay Gillen
Foreword © 2014 Robert P. Moses

This edition © 2014 AK Press (Oakland, Edinburgh, Baltimore).
ISBN: 978-1-84935-199-7 | eBook ISBN: 978-1-84935-200-0
Library of Congress Control Number: 2014940773

AK Press   AK Press
674-A 23rd Street   PO Box 12766
Oakland, CA 94612   Edinburgh EH8 9YE
USA   Scotland
www.akpress.org   www.akuk.com
akpress@akpress.org   ak@akedin.demon.co.uk

The above addresses would be delighted to provide you with the latest AK Press distribution catalog, which features the several thousand books, pamphlets, zines, audio and video products, and stylish apparel published and/or distributed by AK Press. Alternatively, visit our websites for the complete catalog, latest news, and secure ordering.

Cover design by Kate Khatib | manifestor.org/design
Inside cover photos courtesy of The Indigenous Lens Photographic Arts.
Printed in the USA on acid-free paper.

For Paul, Mischa, Sammy, and Matteo

Contents

In a democracy trapped between ideals it intones and practices it condones, Jay Gillen's difficult, profound, unsettling, seminal description encapsulates our national conundrum as, of all things: Pastoral Plays in Mathematics Classes of Schools of Poverty. Because the national conundrum, or drama, has so many layers and twists, Jay has written "program notes," as he calls them, to point the audience toward certain threads in the drama, inviting us to take action. These notes trumpet good news: our national conundrum is not frozen in place, stuff happens, young people—in the past, present, and future—have decided and will decide not to take it anymore.

In Jay's synopsis:

• Underground-Railroad insurgents harbor nineteenth-century runaway slaves,

• Local NAACP insurgents in Mississippi harbor twentieth-century Student Non-Violent Coordinating Committee (SNCC) field secretaries,

• Classrooms of Idealized Algebra Project Students (CIAPs) harbor twenty-first-century education insurgents.

We SNCC field secretaries in the Civil Rights Movement understood how young we were, but as Jay now instructs us, we were no younger than nineteenth-century insurgent runaway slaves, over three-quarters of whom were *also* between thirteen and twenty-nine years of age. Striking, now that these program notes name it: "Of course! It just never occurred to us to think of runaway slaves as a Young People's Project."

Classrooms of Insurgent Algebra Project students organize in the spirit of Ella Baker and, not unlike insurgent runaways and Mississippi SNCCs, position themselves to:

- be central actors
- step into history
- follow their own interests
- get down to and understand root causes
- move the plot along
- face a system that does not lend itself to their needs
- devise means by which to change the system.

Jay, the deep-thought teacher/organizer, reflects aloud about Ella's distinctions:

> Central to Miss Baker's spirit was her insistence that "radical" organizing must get down to the root causes of things. "We not only must *remember* where we have been," she said, "but we must also *understand* where we have been."... You can only understand something that you have dwelt with: talked over, questioned, argued about, thought through, practiced, applied, worked out, acted out, done. The act of understanding, necessarily oral and physical to some extent, never ends. Deeper and deeper and deeper, the same knowledge or "information" burrows and tunnels and seeps into and saturates the soil of your being, till everything you "knew" looks different as you talk with people and do things with them, trying to understand. (Preface, p 10)

Reflection that invites us to reflect in turn on two educational manifestations of our national conundrum:

(1) Schooling tends to treat persons as things, subjects as objects.

Young people, however, reject this treatment. Students in any school can and do participate in the "enormously rich and heroic drama" of the country. "Protected spaces" do exist within which the young people dramatize and drive home their human personhood, with "elaborate style" of language, dress, gesture, and stance, enacting symbolic strategies and plans. Jay's program notes encourage us to interpret insurgent student styles as "pragmatic tools" that help move the action along, preferably in a "desired direction," but in any case, moving the country to change, as young people have done before. Better that than the walking dead.

Situating Classrooms of Insurgent Students in these "protected spaces" links lowly high-school algebra classrooms to the high drama of our national evolving concept of Constitutional personhood. Local NAACP insurgents harbored 1960s SNCC voter registration field secretaries in their private homes, but the much maligned 1957 Civil Rights Act afforded SNCCs a public "crawl space"—partially protected—to enact voter registration organizing: The State of Mississippi locked up SNCC voter registration insurgents, but Civil Rights Division Justice Department Feds held the jail-house key. In that Mississippi Theater of the Civil Rights Movement three constitutional forces were on plain display: (1) Insurgent youth, a "We The People" preamble force, pushed all branches of (2) the Federal Government to regulate (3) State action infringing "the privileges and immunities" of Constitutional People.

It is striking to reflect that it took a full century and three-quarters after the Constitution's preamble was written to acquire federal government "protected spaces," within which SNCC young people could organize insurgent Delta sharecroppers to reclaim an 1870 fifteenth amendment voting right.

Educating for Insurgency frames the country's conundrum as partly about the autonomy of young people.

> We have no consensus as a society about when a small child, maturing into an adult, attains a fully autonomous will and identity. It is clear to most people today, though to fewer people in, say, 1787, that treating Africans as things rather than as persons is an egregious trespass. The case of adolescence is less clear, but young people challenge older adults to think about the consequences of making a mistake in evaluating their autonomy. If it is an error to treat a person as a thing, then it is an error to treat someone who possesses full autonomy as if they do not. (Introduction, p 20–21)

The parallel question of the autonomy of slaves arises in the nation's opening act, the 1787 Constitutional Convention. There, the citizens of several states gather as "We The People," and in Article IV, Section 2, Paragraph 3 tip the Constitutional hat to the former slave James Somerset: "No Person held to Service or Labour in one State, under the Laws thereof, escaping into another, shall, in Consequence of any Law or Regulation therein, be discharged from such Service or Labour, but shall be delivered up on Claim of the Party to whom such Service or Labour may be due." Representatives of the southern states insisted on this clause to counter the effects of the Somerset case, decided fifteen years earlier:

• An African nine year old endures a middle passage in 1749.

• He serves twenty years of personal slavery for Charles Stuart.

• Twenty-nine years old, he accompanies his master to England in 1769.

• He plots his escape into freedom October 1, 1771.

• Slave catchers capture him on November 2, 1771.

• His plot god-mother secures a writ of habeas corpus.

• Judge Mansfield, chief justice of the King's Bench, releases him.

• English planters push a trial to protect the commodities markets.

• June 22, 1772, Judge Mansfield declares James Somerset free.

Thus the Constitution's "Somerset clause" removes American slaveholding from the jurisdiction of English common law—the Play within the Play within the Play that provides a historical marker for this book's second educational manifestation of our national conundrum.

(2) Discussions of the roles of young people generally suffer from a pervasive literalism.

If "Organizing in the Spirit of Ella" animates the discussion about treating persons as things, Ralph Ellison's *Invisible Man* provides similar animation for considering how schools read young people too simplistically:

> To Ellison, surviving as black people in America requires cleverness about how things are not what they seem, of how the contexts of language and history complicate any literal-minded interpretations of things, and make us vulnerable to real dangers if we

ignore their complexities. (Introduction, p 33)

Ellison's protagonist is chastened again and again as his people and the country try to teach him that no words or symbols correspond in any simple way to "reality." (Introduction, p 35)

Charles Stuart was not mature enough as a human being to understand his Constitutional property, James Somerset, whose words and symbols for twenty years, evidently, could not be taken literally. Somerset spent his life telling white folk how to think about the things he knew about. He, seeking freedom, played the role Ralph Ellison gives to the college president, Dr. Bledsoe, who sought, on his own terms, a different concept of freedom: "'I mean it son,' he said. 'I had to be strong and purposeful to get where I am. I had to wait and plan and lick around…Yes, I had to act the nigger!' he said, adding another fiery, 'Yes!'"

Ellison's protagonist, a twentieth century James Somerset incarnation, is staggered by Bledsoe's "disgusting sea of words": "He was looking me in the eye now, his voice charged and sincere, as though uttering a confession, a fantastic revelation which I could neither believe nor deny. Cold drops of sweat moved at a glacier's pace down my spine."

Stuart, the slaveholder, like Ellison's protagonist, could neither believe nor deny the "slave" Somerset's apostasy.

It is an open question whether our country is mature enough to have an honest understanding about the past and present public school education of its youth. Getting down to and understanding the root cause of the education crisis will be no easier than understanding the root cause of "Weapons of Mass Destruction," a task that has proved too much for the Obama Administration and for much if not most of the country. A nation that could neither believe nor deny Secretary of State Colin Powell's fantastic revelation of "Weapons of Mass Destruction"— ignorant and dishonest about root causes—stunned itself into a war of massive "collateral damage."

> Who will have access to knowledge and how, is not a question to be settled once and for all, but the ground of a dramatic contest that we are already engaged in. The action we seek must take no delight in the slaughter or waste of anybody's children, nor refuse consciousness of tragedy and history; rather we must allow ourselves to be affected by what young people in poverty desire and do, so that both we and they may act more gracefully, in more successful courtship. (Part IV, p 170)

Not anybody's children, not even our own.

O, yes, I say it plain,
America never was America to me,
And yet I swear this oath—
America will be!
—Langston Hughes

The intended audience of this book are "practitioners in a system of education that does not yet exist," as Dr. Vincent Harding called us. We are citizens in an America that is yet to become. We are trying to imagine and create a way to educate our children for democracy, but must do this in an America that does not yet know the practice of democracy.

The ideas presented here for creating this new system of education derive from the teaching of Robert Parris Moses, Mississippi field secretary of the Student Nonviolent Coordinating Committee (SNCC) in the 1960s and founder of the Algebra Project. The work of the Algebra Project is to help young people "fashion an insurgency" in the country's educational arrangements, one that will complement the insurgencies in public accommodations and voting rights of the Civil Rights Movement.

My first encounter with this body of work came during a two-week seminar in the summer of 1995 led by Maisha Moses, Bob Moses's daughter, and by Lynn Godfrey, who more than a decade earlier had been Maisha's math teacher in middle school. And their seminar—extending this genealogy—began with a study of

Ella Baker, Bob Moses's teacher, through the reading of an article called, "Organizing in the Spirit of Ella."[1]

Central to Miss Baker's spirit was her insistence that "radical" organizing must get down to the root causes of things. "We not only must *remember* where we have been," she said, "but we must also *understand* where we have been." For almost two decades I have wondered about the difference between "remembering" and "understanding" in Miss Baker's terms.

One of the differences is that you can "remember" something that you have read in a book or that you have been told, but can only "understand" something that you have dwelt with: talked over, questioned, argued about, thought through, practiced, applied, worked out, acted out, done. The act of understanding, necessarily oral and physical to some extent, never ends. Deeper and deeper and deeper, the same knowledge or "information" burrows and tunnels and seeps into and saturates the soil of your being, till everything you "knew" looks different as you talk with people and do things with them, trying to understand.

In addition to following the thinking and practice of Bob Moses, I have tried to imitate the methods of the philosopher and critic Kenneth Burke. Burke's crucial influence on Ralph Ellison has been a growing topic of scholarly investigation.[2] But I first came in contact with Burke through his studies of rhetoric and poetry. He urges us to think about writing as "symbolic action," that

1   Robert P. Moses et al, "The Algebra Project: Organizing in the Spirit of Ella," *Harvard Educational Review* 59/4 (November 1989).

2   See, for example, Bryan Crable, *Ralph Ellison and Kenneth Burke: At the Roots of the Racial Divide.* (Charlottesville and London: University of Virginia Press, 2012).

is, a poem or book *does something* that the writer needs done. Burke's theory of dramatism interprets all human relations as dramatic in form, where we, the players, do things, and react to each other's doing, and come to understand more and more about our roles as we work out our relations with other people and with the world. The parallels and similarities between Burke's dramatism and Moses's Algebra Project are striking and each throws light on the other.

Underlying my argument throughout is the idea that wherever we live or work may be thought of as a self-healing place. "Put down your bucket where you are," Booker T. Washington explained in *Up From Slavery*. And as Dr. Harding taught, the entire history of humankind leads to right here and right now, wherever we find ourselves; and from here and now, constrained but not determined by the past, we are obligated to imagine and create a future that could restore the innocence of the first day.

Keeping the child's innocence before the mind's eye is useful in this regard. So, too, is a saying that Bob Moses quotes. He came upon it on the gravestone of Kingman Brewster, president of Yale University in the 1960s. Brewster's epitaph reads: "The presumption of innocence is not only a legal concept; in common law and in common sense, it requires a generosity of spirit toward the stranger, the expectation of what is best, rather than what is worst, in the other."

The creation of a system of education to foster a true democracy will be founded on this principle. Again and again in my daily work as a teacher in Baltimore, this question of the presumption of innocence is raised. It is raised by the young people; it is raised by their parents; it

is raised by the police, the psychologists, the social workers; it is raised by students wondering if they are safe in
the cafeteria, and by teachers wondering whether they
will lose their jobs.

In our country, slaves were presumed guilty from the
first day. Young people in poverty now are also presumed
guilty in many contexts—treated with suspicion, aver-
sion, alarm, and contempt. The question we explore is not
whether there is justification in reality for these stances.
The question, rather, is what stance we should take toward the young descendants of slaves and their peers in
poverty if we and they presume their innocence, the only
civilized presumption.

We practice taking stances today that will only be
fully appropriate in a future America. There are risks involved in such a practice. Nevertheless, beauty and partial
justice may result, even before the birth of a new world.

Most good teachers of adolescents in schools of poverty feel trapped. We feel unable to meet all the needs of our students, nor can we satisfy the demands of authorities. Most students in these schools feel trapped, too. They spend much of each day doing things they have not free-ly chosen to do, and endure constant judgment and hu-miliation as a matter of course.

This book offers a way past those feelings. It describes a long-term, radical solution to the problem of education in America, one that many teachers, students, and orga-nizers are already working toward, though in ways that have not yet merged into a movement. But it also pres-ents an immediate way to understand, picture, and talk about what we human beings are doing in these strange places, so that we can feel less trapped and work more positively and hopefully.

Although I use some abstract, theoretical, and often literary ideas to develop this understanding and picture, the descriptions below are in one way just a case study, highlighting the actual practices of a student-led orga-nization called the Baltimore Algebra Project. We have found, using this way of understanding our work, that other feelings and actions have emerged to fight toe to toe with the feelings of being trapped: sometimes joy or comfort, sometimes political or organizing work, some-times the thrill of intellectual exploration and discovery, sometimes the sense of being connected to the whole river of the freedom struggle, to its legacy of courage, endurance, and hope.

A how-to guide would be nice. But this book should be read more like program notes at a play. It gives some background and context, hints at the life stories of some of the actors, focuses the viewer's attention on potentially important themes or images, and generally aims to make the experience of the play's performance more intimate, significant, and enjoyable. The play is the students' lives and our work in schools. The reader's role, as audience or actor, is left for you to decide.

In the middle of the last century, public secondary schools were conceived to operate as factories, churning out workers adapted to the demands of assembly lines and industrial bureaucracies and to the consumption of products made in factories. Today, the dominant analogy is that schools should be like the laboratories of scientists, experimenting with initial conditions and inputs, controlling for specified variables, to induce brain-states adapted to the demands of an economy structured by scientists and the consumption of digitized products. In the public schools of relatively comfortable adolescents, these ways of thinking have worked well enough to produce the necessary workers and consumers for the bourgeoisie to go about their business.

But in schools for adolescents in poverty, and particularly for the descendants of slaves, both the factory and laboratory analogies are inadequate. Neither the young people themselves, nor their parents, nor their teachers have been able to look through these frames and make much sense of what they see. The factory schools couldn't prepare students for factory jobs that no longer existed. And today's "experimental design," "data-driven," "evidence-based" schools leave the great majority of African American and poor students unable to take math or science courses for credit in college, and so qualify them only for service jobs that robots will probably be doing a few years from now.

We need a way of describing and thinking about public schools of poverty that addresses what actually happens as opposed to what the dominant ideology says should happen. In general terms we are looking for a frame that accomplishes two related tasks: First, our mode of description and analysis must help us understand the bewildering experience of being a student, teacher, or parent trying to do something human in schools of poverty. These schools literally make many of us ill. We become so infuriated, depressed, impatient, confused, revolted, thwarted, humiliated, as we try to act on our own behalf or on behalf of others that both young people and adults often develop physical symptoms of disease. And while we are experiencing the physical and emotional symptoms of striving for life in a place that doesn't fit our humanity, we hear the constant drumbeat of propaganda that there is something wrong with *us*, not with the place. The terms of the propaganda—"data," "objectives," "mandates," "test scores," "protocols," "requirements," "deadlines," "evaluations"—flood our consciousness until it is hard to hear our own voices or to use our own names for things. It becomes difficult to make ourselves understood, as if we were babbling, because the distance between our experience and the official "reality" grows greater and greater. At this point, one of three things happens: we are labeled by the authorities as "defiant" or "insubordinate" and forced to leave; we decide on our own to leave to preserve our health and sanity; or we compromise and accept the ideology of schooling whenever we must, shutting off our humanity into smaller and smaller boxes alienated from any concept of the common good.

So one task that a better frame will accomplish is to give us words, images, and ways of thinking that are sturdy and agile enough to do battle with the propaganda of the dominant ideology as manifested in schools. It will let us survive in schools of poverty without being forced out or forced to compromise or made ill.

The second task is to prepare for an insurgency of young people. That is, we are looking for a description and analysis that is pragmatically constructive. If our frame doesn't help us decide how to transform the world, in Paolo Freire's terms, it is too weak.[1] We postulate that the principal agents of the transformation will be the students and define our ultimate goal as an insurgency led by young people in poverty.

By "insurgency" we mean to emphasize the insufficiency of parliamentary, electoral, or technical procedures, and to describe instead a rising up of young people that massively interrupts the functioning of the country's educational system and forces a rearrangement of roles, authority, and power well beyond the boundaries of "school." The degree of disruption will need to be greater than during the insurgency that forced changes to the country's electoral system, because the right to education is a more fundamental cultural function than the right to vote. As explained below, white middle-class parents (followed by middle-class parents of color) reacted to the changes brought on in the 1950s and 1960s by finding new ways to separate their children from children growing up in different castes. Jim Crow lost its grip on public

---

1   Paolo Freire, *Pedagogy of the Oppressed* (New York: Herder and Herder, 1970).

accommodations and voting rights, but keeps education firmly segregated by race and caste; much more disruption, therefore, will be needed before this final breakthrough occurs.

The educational insurgency will certainly use parliamentary, electoral, or technical demands and procedures as organizing tools, but those demands and procedures are not the aims of the insurgency. For example, this book describes a demand for math literacy—but as an organizing tool, not as an end in itself. Often tactics such as this are confused for ends, but the possibility of confusion is one of the reasons math literacy, for example, was chosen as a demand. There is a consensus among nearly all elements of society that math literacy is good in itself; therefore organizing for math literacy among poor students of color is permitted by institutional authorities. We argue that the cover given by this consensus and the authority earned by doing math create opportunities for students in poverty to organize massive interruptions of the educational and social system. Similarly, voter registration was not radical in 1960; there was a wide consensus that voter registration was a good thing. But voter registration among sharecroppers in Mississippi was radical, and resulted in massive interruptions of the Southern, and eventually of the national, political and social systems.

The Marxist frame—that schools reproduce class structures—is certainly helpful to an extent. Samuel Bowles and Herbert Gintis give a detailed explication of how educational reproduction works in America.[2] The limitation of the Marxist frame, however, is that we will

---

2   Samuel Bowles and Herbert Gintis, *Schooling in Capitalist America* (New York: Basic Books, 1977).

need to wait until the revolution for schooling's role in the reproduction of class dynamics to change. There is an important body of work that understands working-class young people as resistant to the reproduction of class in schools. Part I of this book centers on a particular interpretation of this resistance in the context of the black freedom struggle in America. But understanding the students as resistant is not quite enough to help us understand how they will become educated in a pre-revolutionary era.

The problem is chicken and egg. To the extent that schooling simply reproduces existing class dynamics, no changes in how schooling works will matter till class dynamics change. But class dynamics are unlikely to change until a revolutionary or insurrectionary consciousness develops among the young—and their consciousness develops largely through schooling.

The obvious solution to this problem is to reduce the scale of the task. Subversive parents try to raise subversive children. African nationalists try to raise African nationalist children at the scale of the family or on the somewhat larger scale of a cultural organization or church, for example. The approach to creating a mini-society that will reproduce specific human dynamics can sometimes be extended to the size of a private or charter school. Such schools try to insulate children from the oppressive forces that determine the shape of schooling as an unhelpful or degrading institution. Some small schools of this kind have been relatively successful in giving children and adolescents an experience of human interaction that is very different from the norm. Some have been less successful.

The example of positive mini-societies nevertheless demonstrates that the Marxist view of cultural reproduction is not the last word on how children grow up.

Though schools do reproduce oppressive relations, there are potential paths through which small trickles of something different may leak out, until a larger revolution or insurgency takes root.

The question this book explores is how to understand the actual dynamics of public schools of poverty in such a way that potent mini-societies can be created right inside them. The charter or private school is one route. But the great mass of oppressed young people are in normative public high schools. That mass possesses almost unfathomable energy. We want to develop a frame through which their energy could become foregrounded not only as unorganized resistance, but as actually constructing an insurgency.

To understand the terms and ways of thinking presented here, it is important to reflect on two particular inadequacies of the dominant ideology as it relates to education. (1) Schooling tends to treat persons as things, subjects as objects; (2) discussions of the roles of young people generally suffer from a pervasive literalism.

Treating persons as things is an ethical error analyzed over millennia in many different cultures. Capitalism or the West or Whiteness are particularly egregious violators in this mode: we have regularly bought and sold human beings and continue to monetize everything we can name. Another way to understand the ethical error of treating persons as things is to consider certain traditional forms of thinking that refuse to treat even animals, plants, mountains, or rivers as mere things. Thanking the buffalo or the bear for their meat, cherishing the returning rain or sun, are "superstitions" to "scientific" minds, but in other ways of thinking these are acts that establish our own humanity: it is an ethical requirement to be conscious and aware of our relations to the world, to be "in relation" to the world as opposed to merely using it. Though this traditional awareness may go too far for many of us brought up differently, it highlights the distinction between parts of the world toward which we hold ethical obligations and parts of the world toward which we don't. In western terms, this distinction is between "persons" and "things."

The factory or laboratory analogies and the everyday practice in schools of poverty encourage this ethical error. Young people are often objectified, and young people whose ancestors were slaves, legal property that a person could own, may be especially sensitive, at least emotionally, to such a category mistake. In general, however, the disregard for young people's full personhood is taken for granted. This is explored in detail below. For now, we simply point out that in the official, normative view, young people are of doubtful personhood. Unlike adults, their will and identity are not thought to be fully autonomous. Having committed no crime, having made no positive choice to participate in any organization or institution, adolescents are compelled wholesale to attend schools and to follow school rules, or they are humiliated and punished. This is a condition generally not suffered by persons officially categorized as autonomous.

We have no consensus as a society about when a small child, maturing into an adult, attains a fully autonomous will and identity. It is clear, however, to most people today, far more than in, say, 1787, that treating Africans as things rather than as persons is an egregious trespass. The case of adolescence is less clear, but young people challenge older adults to think about the consequences of making a mistake in evaluating their autonomy. If it is an error to treat a person as a thing, then it is an error to treat someone who possesses full autonomy as if they do not. For many years women, of course, had trouble convincing men of the strength of this argument, and in much of the world still do. With regard to young people, the case is still far from obvious, especially in schools of poverty, and pushing the point is one of the aims of this book.

The second major inadequacy in most discussions of education is an unfortunate literalism. Literalism is the idea that words refer directly or transparently to things in the world, and that confusion in communication can be eliminated by simply finding the right words to represent any intended meaning.[3] Language, however, is less straightforward than literal-minded people would wish. Words are full of overtones and undertones, shadings and associations, and they carry immensely complicated histories with them wherever they go. We call speakers "tone-deaf" who seem oblivious to how context might modify, limit, or expand the significations of the

---

3   Jonathan Swift describes the literalism of the Great Academy of Lagado in *Gulliver's Travels:* "An expedient was therefore offered, 'that since words are only names for things, it would be more convenient for all men to carry about them such things as were necessary to express a particular business they are to discourse on.'...[M]any of the most learned and wise adhere to the new scheme of expressing themselves by things; which has only this inconvenience attending it, that if a man's business be very great, and of various kinds, he must be obliged, in proportion, to carry a greater bundle of things upon his back, unless he can afford one or two strong servants to attend him. I have often beheld two of those sages almost sinking under the weight of their packs, like pedlars among us, who, when they met in the street, would lay down their loads, open their sacks, and hold conversation for an hour together; then put up their implements, help each other to resume their burdens, and take their leave."

words they use. Consider, for example, the Columbia Law School trustee who recently asked a black applicant interviewing for admission: "If *you* say 'people of color,' what's wrong with *my* saying 'colored people'?" The literalist is baffled by the distinction, while anyone with a sense of how history intertwines with language will understand that the stylistic choice between "people of color" and "colored people" today, in 2013, communicates something about the speaker's stance and values.

Much of the language used by schools of poverty—or by bureaucracies or researchers about schools—suffers from the stylistic defect of literalism. I argue in accordance with a long rhetorical tradition that the stylistic defect is actually an ethical defect. Tone-deafness in speech often goes hand in hand with cruelty in action. The trustee who has trouble distinguishing between "people of color" and "colored people" is likely to reinforce the institutionalized cruelties of racism.

But the argument goes far beyond the political correctness of specific terms. The rhetorical tradition we are invoking advances a strategic approach toward language as symbolic action. The bad style of school bulletins on truancy or test protocols, or the bad style of most official "standards" describing curriculum or behavior, abet and enforce reactionary attitudes toward the struggle of young people in poverty. This point is discussed explicitly in Part II on teaching *Brown vs. Board* in a segregated school, and is relevant throughout. Actual or pretended ignorance about how our official language clatters against reality is in itself a kind of wrong-doing and contributes to making schools of poverty unlivable for human beings.

But even more important is the converse: sophisticated and even "literary" appreciation for *good* style is potentially helpful in directing us toward good and humane action inside of schools, and can help us dig in and survive there. What we find as we explore this topic is that human beings are naturally graceful and sensitive to the complexity of the symbols and language they use. We find that young people are almost obsessed with stylistic nuance and shading—in language, dress, gesture, or stance. And we find that any elaborate series of stylistic choices can add up to a strategy for action, to a way of taking on the world as it presents itself to us, and possibly of transforming it.

The more literal-minded we are, the more we will despair of getting out from under the bureaucratic mass. But using and appreciating language that is multi-layered and alive can give us a different perspective. If we understand the roles of young people in schools of poverty as part of an enormously rich and heroic drama rather than simply despairing at their mistakes or at our mistakes or at the administrations' mistakes, we will be much more hopeful. We can take a bit of the action and language and interpret it; and then we can apply or try out our interpretation on another bit and see if it helps us make sense of something that was troubling us. This sort of functional interpretation then becomes a pragmatic tool that actually helps move the action along in a desired direction. Through public speech and action attached in an aesthetically sophisticated way to radical traditions of speaking and acting, we may find ourselves "stepping into history," making things happen.

By resolutely treating persons as persons, not as things, and by celebrating and putting to use the historical and aesthetic complexities of public speech and action, we counter the ersatz "science" of the education world. Bad "science" tries to expunge ethical categories from its descriptions and procedures. "Scientists" claim that they have no horse in the race, and only want to know the facts. This is ignorant or disingenuous. Science, like all human inventions, contributes to human purposes, but those purposes are not determined scientifically. How we act toward each other, the field of ethics and the beginning of politics, results from our attitudes, habits, and decisions, not exclusively from observable data. We all know this, of course, but the pose of determining action "scientifically" from data alone is often authoritative in twenty-first-century America. The authority of "science" will pass, but in the meantime we who believe in freedom should heap up barricades from whatever materials we can find to create protected regions that operate under a different authority.

In designing our barricades, I look to two deeply thought out and long-practiced traditions. They may not seem on their face to be traditions of education, but they are rooted in education nonetheless.

The first is the organizing tradition of Ella Baker, Bob Moses, and the Student Non-violent Coordinating Committee (SNCC). This tradition is exceedingly old and is beautifully described by Bernice Johnson Reagon, another disciple of Ella Baker, in a chapter called "The African American Congregational Song Tradition" from *If You Don't Go, Don't Hinder Me*:

> In congregational singing, there is no soloist, there are only songleaders. The difference between a soloist and a songleader is that with a soloist, they have a part by themselves and, if there are other voices, they are in a part of the background. With a songleader,

you can start a song, but you cannot give it life without the participation of other voices. You may have
verses, or you may have a call with others responding,
but there is no sense that you could stand by yourself.
Songleaders get nowhere unless the congregation
takes the song over as its own—then the songleader
has something to do, a song to lead, a song to move
to another level. Songleaders can start the song, but
they cannot finish it.[4]

Robert Parris Moses, born and raised in Harlem,
a young math teacher and student of philosophy, went
south in 1960 with a letter of introduction from Bayard
Rustin to Ella Baker to get started on some civil rights
work. At the time, Miss Baker was the Executive Di-
rector of the Southern Christian Leadership Conference
(SCLC), Martin Luther King, Jr.'s organization, a co-
alition of black ministers. Ella Baker had already been
active in radical circles for thirty years, creating worker
cooperatives, developing grassroots leadership for the
NAACP, and connecting activists across the country.
When Bob Moses met her at the SCLC, however, she
was frustrated for a number of reasons. In his book, *Radical Equations,* Moses writes that "her style strained an
already uncomfortable political relationship and finally made it impossible for Miss Baker to continue with
SCLC. 'She wasn't church,' one SCLC minister said. She
wasn't deferential. She wasn't a man in an organization
that was patriarchal as well as hierarchical. And what I
think was probably the most critical tension: her concept

4   Bernice Johnson Reagon, *If You Don't Go, Don't Hinder Me:
The African American Sacred Song Tradition* (Lincoln: University of Nebraska Press, 2001), 63–64.

of leadership, that it should emerge from the community and be helped in its growth by grassroots organizers, clashed with SCLC's idea of projecting and protecting a single charismatic leader."[5]

In 1960, Miss Baker convened young people of the sit-in movement at the founding of the Student Nonviolent Coordinating Committee and urged them to let their new organization take root independently of the older adults running the SCLC and the NAACP. The young people had to figure things out on their own. They had to believe in their own ability to lead. They had to find motivation for action through their own experiences, discussions, and decisions, without requiring sanction from anyone else, if they were to bear up under the onslaught white America had in store for them. Their discipline was not to be the discipline of an army that follows a chain of command from generals down. Their discipline conformed to a different tradition: the discipline of communal responsibilities among peers who consciously agree to share a common purpose and way of living.

Organizers are crucial to the tradition represented by Miss Baker and Bob Moses. The organizers know it is hard to excavate a common purpose out of all the different tendencies, needs, and views any collection of people has, especially when the pressure merely to survive is very great. The organizers also know that it is hard for people to remember their own power, since most of us are only too happy to surrender our power to charismatic leaders who will just tell us what to do. But effective organizers like Bob Moses and Ella Baker succeed in helping people

---

5   Robert P. Moses and Charles E. Cobb, *Radical Equations: Civil Rights from Mississippi to the Algebra Project* (Boston: Beacon Press, 2001), 33–34.

define a consensus about what they are working on, what they are trying to do, and also succeed in establishing structures whereby a group with a consensus about what their work is can organize themselves to get it done.

When Bob Moses found himself in Mississippi, the consensus turned out to be around voting rights, and the structure turned out to be voter registration drives, the Freedom Summer campaign and the Mississippi Freedom Democratic Party. Many histories have been written about this work because it affected the lives of millions, and still affects us today. The right to vote is not a radical enough goal, but it was the issue a consensus developed around and therefore became a powerful organizing tool. Organizers and theoreticians might think they know more than the people, but it takes time for the people to learn to trust themselves, paths may be winding, and unexpected, powerful things may happen on the way. Trying to short-circuit the winding path to communal learning usually backfires, because the "experts," charismatic leaders, or vanguards take up the space that the people must learn to structure for themselves. Voting rights was an organizing tool, not an end goal. Thousands of sharecroppers, day laborers, and domestic workers in Mississippi were willing to risk their lives for the right to vote, and that willingness created the opportunity for a mass movement that had previously been impossible to grow in the Deep South. Others who prefer to focus on different goals must not only articulate why their preference makes sense, but must also find a way to get people to risk their lives for it.

For Ella Baker and Bob Moses what is more radical than voting rights is education. The Civil War had the effect of freeing the slaves and making them citizens, but "education," Moses says, "is the subtext of the right to vote." Citizenship, due process, protection under the law, and the right to vote hold little meaning without full access to the benefits of education. More importantly, the viability of an oppressed population as a culture and people is inextricably linked to the way its children are raised, to their control of how young people are brought up and for what purposes. And this question is not one to be answered top-down. It is a question whose answers must emerge from the oppressed community, helped by organizers to develop consensus and structures that will get the work of education done. In the process of this struggle, the members of more powerful castes will fight viciously to preserve their own children's status, even more viciously than they fight to preserve other privileges. The more powerful castes understand that pressure on the nation's educational arrangements is pressure on their way of life.

Obviously, teachers will play a crucial role in giving birth to the required consensus and structures for a liberated system of education. In fact, it is becoming harder and harder to distinguish the role of teacher in a school of poverty from the role of organizer. We start each year in the standardized school with no consensus at all among our students about what we are there for. No common purpose; no sense of a shared task freely undertaken; no agreement on how our work should be structured beyond the idiotic routines of drills, course requirements, tests, and grades. In these circumstances, if we see our students as persons not as things, our first responsibility in the Baker/Moses tradition is to start to develop a consensus with our students and their families about what our work is. This is easier said than done.

What follows throughout this book is an approach to understanding the organizing task of developing such a consensus and then putting it to work. Guided by this tradition, we were actually somewhat surprised to notice ourselves accomplishing what we set out to do, and are still trying to understand exactly how we did it. This book is a part of that effort.

Bob Moses points out that, through an "accident of history," math teachers in particular find themselves having to accept the role of organizer today. No consensus about education can avoid the significance of abstract symbolic languages in controlling power in the twenty-first century. Put another way, no community will voluntarily accept a system of education that leaves its young people without access to sophisticated quantitative reasoning, because that lack of access so obviously corresponds today to a lower caste status. The point of mathematical literacy is not that everyone must be a mathematician, just as the point of verbal literacy does not entail that everyone must be a poet or professional writer. The point is that as a practical fact of organizing around education for equality, the ability to understand and evaluate quantitative arguments represented in abstract symbolic forms cannot be left out: no community will allow it.

Appreciating this "accident of history" and his own fortuitous position as both a Harvard-trained philosopher of mathematics and accomplished organizer on a national scale, Bob Moses began the Algebra Project in 1982. The Algebra Project works explicitly in the tradition of Ella Baker, helping teachers, parents, and students develop a consensus about how young people in poverty should be brought up, and working to create structures through which young people and their families can organize themselves to get what they need. We formulate this goal as helping young people fashion their own insurgency, an insurgency that will be even more disruptive than SNCC's, insofar as ending Jim Crow education is more radical than voting.

In the Baltimore Algebra Project, we have spent fifteen years building a student organization that uses math literacy as an organizing tool. High school students and recent graduates run their own non-profit business from an off-campus office, using SNCC as a model for collective decision-making. Public schools and after-school agencies contract with the students for peer-to-peer math literacy services based at the schools, and other non-profits are increasingly hiring Baltimore Algebra Project youth to teach their organizations to be more youth-governed. Over ten years, Baltimore high school students and recent graduates, nearly all black, have earned millions of dollars through their producer co-op. And doing math—tutoring, running summer math programs and after-school study groups, organizing peer teaching in classrooms—creates an economic base for the young people to do political work, too. The relatively lucrative and marketable business of math subsidizes student committees that advance organizing goals.

The political work is of three kinds. First, there is the students' work in running their own organization. They have developed a culture and mechanisms of self-governance that fit their needs and that are sound enough to earn the respect of customers and investors outside the organization. Second, the same students have led or joined concrete campaigns around their material conditions—transportation, youth incarceration, school funding—and have won major victories. Third, they are learning about building coalitions with other organizations at both the local and national levels, gradually developing an awareness of the larger world and larger strategic issues, and learning how to pass that larger awareness on to new generations of youth coming up.

The purpose of this book is not, however, to tell that story in detail. It is rather to lay out an understanding of young people's roles and of the teacher/organizer role that makes the story of youth organizing possible. It is about a way of seeing and talking about our experiences in schools of poverty that lets us do our work without being demoralized or forced out.

People who see Baltimore Algebra Project youth operating in public contexts are often startled. Depending on the observer's perspective, they can be either pleasantly or unpleasantly surprised. But in either case, the surprise comes from the young people's clear and conscious refusal of the role of "prop." They step into history as persons, and observers find themselves required to re-act to their humanity, to figure out what relation they are going to have with these forceful young people. At the root of the Baker/Moses organizing tradition is the conviction that every human being is a person who can decide to step into history, which is an act that puts you into dynamic relation with other persons, and that makes human arrangements different from what they would have been without you. Things, props, mere objects, play no such role in history.

The second major tradition I use in this book is a tradition of verbal study that goes under the heading "rhetoric," and for which my principal authorities are Kenneth Burke and Ralph Ellison. The word "rhetoric" has unfortunately narrowed in common use to describe verbal tricks deployed to bias or twist public opinion in ways that distract attention from "logic" and "facts." But in the tradition represented by Burke and Ellison, "rhetoric" refers to any use of speech designed "to induce action in beings that by nature respond to symbols." Logic, by this tradition, is not opposed to rhetoric, but is a part of rhetoric. Sometimes the arguments we make to induce action in others are strictly logical arguments. More often our appeals are directed at least in part toward the emotions of a listener, or are intended to help an audience identify our argument with someone they admire or with the type of person they would like to become. This rhetorical tradition treats our susceptibility to various forms of persuasion as one of the key facts about human beings: we are a species that responds not only to logic, but to emotion and to both conscious and unconscious identifications as well. There are traditions in many cultures that treasure thinking and teaching about how to use these various means to induce action in others through the use of verbal or other symbols, and especially about how to induce right action, action that tends toward the common good.

The field of rhetoric interpreted in this way is vast. But I am interested in it for a relatively specific purpose: in what ways do people in schools—young and old—seek to induce action in others through the use of symbols (that is both through language and through nonverbal symbolic action)? We are looking at this, following Burke and Ellison, from many points of view: not only how teachers or administrators speak and act so that the students will be persuaded to act in certain ways; but also how the students speak and act to induce actions in each other and in the teachers and administrators as well.

An approach through this rhetorical tradition is intended to systematically undo the bad effects of literalism in thinking about schools. To the literal-minded, a lesson on writing an essay or on DNA is simply about writing an essay or DNA. The state assigns certain "content" to be "taught" and the teacher then "delivers" the content. But to a student of rhetoric, these lessons are complex symbolic acts in contexts rich with meaning, saturated with the purposes of both the teachers and the students and with the purposes of people far from the classroom who have induced the students and teachers to participate in the lesson in the first place.

Any page of Ellison's great novel, *Invisible Man*, is an exercise in this kind of rhetorical study. To Ellison, surviving as black people in America requires cleverness about how things are not what they seem, about how the contexts of language and history complicate any literal-minded interpretations of things, and make us vulnerable to real dangers if we ignore their complexities. The narrator of *Invisible Man* is constantly discovering that there is no meaning independent of context, that the world, as he puts it, is less "solid" than he thought, though he nevertheless holds onto the search for right interpretations because he will die without them.

In a traumatic scene, his college president, Dr. Bledsoe, expels him from the school, saying:

> "You're nobody, son. You don't exist—can't you see that? The white folk tell everybody what to think— except men like me. I tell *them*; that's my life telling white folk how to think about the things I know about. Shocks you, doesn't it? Well that's the way it is. It's a nasty deal and I don't always like it myself. But

you listen to me: I didn't make it and I know I can't change it. But I've made my place in it and I'll have every Negro in the country hanging on tree limbs by morning if it means staying where I am."

He was looking me in the eye now, his voice charged and sincere, as though uttering a confession, a fantastic revelation which I could neither believe nor deny. Cold drops of sweat moved at a glacier's pace down my spine....

"A man gets old winning his place, son. So you go ahead, go tell your story; match your truth against my truth. The broader truth."[6]

Ellison's narrator stops paying attention. "I no longer listened, nor saw more than the play of light upon the metallic disks of his glasses, which now seemed to float within the disgusting sea of his words. Truth, truth, what was truth? Nobody I knew, not even my own mother, would believe me if I tried to tell them. Nor would I tomorrow, I thought, nor would I."[7]

The meanings in *Invisible Man* are dizzying, but no more dizzying than those faced in America's schools of poverty. The ironies, the unreliability of pronouncements, the mirrors within mirrors that confuse reality and appearance—these conditions are our normal state. In Ellison's story, we have a school administrator punishing a student apparently to ensure his own standing with the white power brokers who lend him authority. Should the narrator believe that the exemplary president of the college is so self-hating, has so internalized hatred

---

6   Ralph Ellison, *Invisible Man*, (New York: Vintage International, 1995), 143–144.

7   Ibid., 144.

of his own people? Or is this only a stance the president assumes to advance his interests rationally in the racist context? Hard to believe the first interpretation; hard to believe the second. "I could neither believe nor deny," the narrator concludes.

And how can we convey in any definite way the nightmarish intricacies of confusion and vertigo induced by dysfunctional schools. No one believes the young people when they try to tell the simple truth about their experience. They are doubted and distrusted from the moment they walk in the doors. And it is difficult for them even to believe themselves the next day.

Ellison's protagonist is chastened again and again as his people and the country try to teach him that no words or symbols correspond in any simple way to "reality." "I've come a long way from those days when, full of illusion, I lived a public life and attempted to function under the assumption that the world was solid and all the relationships therein. Now I know men are different and that all life is divided and that only in division is there true health."

If we are going to have an effect on the world through our speech and action, we will have to learn to build health from confusing division. Health will not come from any literalist instructions or commands, but rather from complex, ambiguous terms in fluid and ever-changing combinations.

This is actually what human beings do, and in particular what Africans in America have been doing from the start. The crucial black cultural forms that function as tools for survival are spectacularly allusive, multivalent, and elaborate as symbolic systems: music, folklore, folk art, dance, and verbal inventiveness are immense cultural achievements now permeating the whole world's culture, and they are in no way literal-minded.

In struggling to create his novel from the ground of black culture, Ellison turned to the work of his friend and mentor, Kenneth Burke. Burke was developing a theory of "dramatism," the understanding of human motivation through the elements of drama. The protagonist's remark that "all life is divided and only in division is there true health" could have been lifted from Burke's *A Rhetoric of Motives*, which Ellison was reading as he composed *Invisible Man*.[8] In a section titled "A metaphorical view of hierarchy," Burke writes:

> So the myth of society's return to the child, or the child's return to the womb, or the womb's return to the sea, can all point towards a myth still farther back, the myth of a power prior to all parturition. Then divided things were not yet proud in the private property of their divisiveness. Division was still but "enlightenment"....
>
> Partition provides *terms*; thereby it allows the parts to comment on one another. But this "loving" relation allows also for the "fall" into terms antagonistic in their partiality, until dialectically resolved by reduction to "higher" terms.[9]

Burke and Ellison work the vein of rhetorical tradition that accepts the necessity of division—terms for and against, dizzy meanings heading off in all directions—but that seeks to harness division and fragments of meaning

---

8   See Bryan Crable, *Ralph Ellison and Kenneth Burke: At the Roots of the Racial Divide*, 79–111.

9   Kenneth Burke, *A Rhetoric of Motives* (Berkeley: University of California, 1969/1950), 140.

for common purposes and common ends. Burke's guiding analogy for this approach to understanding human action is the genre of drama. A play necessarily divides competing principles between characters that battle and strive with each other. Within the play, one character or another may come out on top, but seen from a different vantage point, the roles of the opposing characters contribute together and collaborate in a common aesthetic purpose—the effect of the play as a whole.

Somehow or other, we must come to understand the roles of young people in this way. We must try to conceive of a unity of action where the young people, being themselves, contribute not to the state's ends, but to an end worked out in the common good. The underlying difficulty is that schools of poverty necessarily bring together people of fundamentally different statuses in the social hierarchy: adults and youth; the educated and the uneducated; middle-class teachers and working-class youth; and increasingly, white teachers and students of color. Fortunately, the Burke/Ellison rhetorical tradition is especially useful in studying communication between different kinds within complex hierarchies. In literal terms, the powerful simply have power and the powerless do not. This is what makes us feel so trapped in schools. But in the imagined world of a play, both the powerful and the powerless contribute to the movement of the plot, influencing each other, and contributing to a totality that is beyond the absolute control of either party.

Once we understand young people as genuinely equal actors in the drama of the nation, not as pawns or victims or props, many more possibilities will begin to come to mind for entering the action and moving it along toward insurrection. In fact, they are moving us along already.

PART I

The Political Role of Young People in Schools of Poverty

In 1772, at the Court of the King's Bench in London, Lord Chief Justice Mansfield agreed with the American fugitive James Somerset that he was a free man and not the property of his master. The slave's act of self-emancipation produced anxiety, argument, counter-argument, and increased movement toward rebellion across the Atlantic in the American colonies.[1] Lord Mansfield declared property in human beings to be so "odious" a concept that it could not be countenanced by common law, and was nowhere established in the positive acts of Parliament. Slaveholders in the colonies consequently feared that their slaves would attempt to free themselves as well, and that they would seek and find protection in King George's courts. By 1776, British encouragement of slave rebellions had proceeded far enough as both a political and military strategy that the Declaration of Independence includes reference to the King's "excit[ing] domestic insurrection among us" as

---

1 Alfred Blumrosen and Ruth Blumrosen, *Slave Nation: How Slavery United the Nation and Sparked the American Revolution* (Naperville, Illinois: Sourcebooks, 2005); Robert P. Moses, "Constitutional Property v. Constitutional People," in *Quality Education As a Constitutional Right: Creating a Grassroots Movement to Transform Public Schools,* edited by Theresa Perry et al (Boston: Beacon Press, 2010).

one of the colonists' reasons for creating a new nation.[2] Fear of runaway slaves was so important a motive for the revolution that the southern states insisted in 1787 on Article IV, Section 2 of the Constitution, requiring the return of fugitives to their masters. If the states with few slaves would not agree to treat fugitives as property, the states with more slaves were prepared to forego the advantages of political union.

The Constitution, of course, did not settle the issue; slaves ran away despite its provisions. From the Revolution to the Civil War, again and again, the acts of slaves seeking their freedom provoked conflicts between white people: suits for the return of runaways; trials of those who protected runaways; the abolition movement itself, fueled by the fact and narratives of fugitive slaves and by their active participation in the agitation and struggle against slavery. The Fugitive Slave Act of 1850, a final step before war, caused intense escalation of conflicts between competing factions of white people as they tried to position themselves in response to the self-liberating acts of slaves. In 1854, for example, the liberation of nineteen-year-old Anthony Burns, who had fled from captivity in Virginia to freedom in Massachusetts, resulted in a national political crisis. When federal authorities in Boston attempted to enforce the Fugitive Slave Act by returning Burns to his master, thousands of both white and black abolitionists took to the streets, surrounding the federal courthouse. The mayor of Boston imposed martial law, and the President of the United States, Franklin Pierce, authorized the dispatch of US Marines to assist in returning the fugitive to Virginia.

---

2   David Waldstreicher, *Slavery's Constitution: From Revolution to Ratification* (New York: Hill and Wang, 2009), 41.

Each insurgent act of running away, or of poisoning or arson or violence against a slaveholder, had its own origins in the mind and body of the slave.[3] Sometimes the unit of insurgency was a single person; sometimes a pair or small group; sometimes a band, or even scores or several hundreds in the case of the larger rebellions. Eventually, a complex network developed to support the insurgent runaways—the Underground Railroad—that might be thought of in certain cases as just several houses or farms or churches on a particular route north and, in other cases, as a whole system of communication and material assistance. All these manifestations and effects of the intention to be free hinged on each individual slave's understanding of his or her own interests—not the interests of the slaveholder, not the interests of the northern sympathizer, but the slave's interests. They acted, and white people with their hands on the levers of power were unable to ignore the altered circumstances caused by the insurgent slaves' actions. Powerful people re-acted to the deliberate, consequential, voluntary movements of the less powerful, expending incalculable energy in debate, publication, assembly, argument, legislation, material assistance or material obstruction, culminating in four years of mutual maiming and slaughter, none of which would have followed from a slave population that was merely docile and inert.

The great majority of fugitive slaves were young, roughly seventy-five percent between the ages of thirteen and twenty-nine.[4] Most histories do not clearly identify

---

3   Vincent Harding, *There Is A River: The Black Struggle for Freedom in America* (San Diego: Harcourt Brace, 1981).

4   John Hope Franklin and Loren Schweninger, *Runaway Slaves: Rebels on the Plantation* (New York, Oxford: Oxford University Press), 210.

these young people as having played a central political role in the country's sectional conflict or in the development of its constitutional principles. Many historians consider the maneuvers of statesmen who were enacting laws, making speeches, publishing arguments, and giving orders, or of the voters and economic interests to which these states-men responded. Others discuss economic and legal struc-tures, capital and labor markets, geography, technology, literature, journalism, and so on. But the political role of the fugitive slave should be understood as central.[5] Each act of running away was a fully moral act, whether or not the fugitive considered or was even aware of the legal and political arguments of the powerful. And fully moral acts always carry political implications; that is, they necessarily raise questions of who has power and who does not.

The uncontrolled movements of young people in poverty today, and particularly of the descendants of slaves, generate debates about educational "reform" in much the same way that the uncontrolled movements of their insurgent ancestors generated debates about the status of slavery before the Civil War.

The indocility of young people in high schools, for example, provokes tensions and hardening of positions around school discipline and policing. The concept of

---

5   "By the 1850s runaways had become a major source of sectional antagonism *solely* because of the political con-flict they both exposed and provoked. Far more directly than abolitionist propaganda, fugitive slaves forced both the North and South into ever hardening defenses of their conflicting social structures….Yet because slaves influ-enced the polity indirectly, as outsiders, the debate over slavery rarely centered on slave resistance as such." James Oakes, "The Political Significance of Slave Resistance." *History Workshop Journal* 22 (October 1986), 89–107.

"zero tolerance" feeds on the fear of insubordination, violence, and defiance; but the harshness of zero-tolerance policies provokes the outraged reactions of civil libertarians, of some parents, and of a certain kind of child advocate. This dynamic—sometimes articulated as between "permissiveness" and "structure" or between "freedom" and "order"—plays out again and again in schools as in the larger society. Here we are stressing the necessary contribution to this dynamic of the young people's stubborn agency. Just as it was necessary that slaves stubbornly ran away in the antebellum south for there to be a controversy at all about the legal status of the runaway, so the education wars depend for their existence on the stubborn indocility of students in poverty and especially of descendants of slaves today. The Department of Education rewards states that fire teachers whose students have certain test results. The teachers and their allies demonstrate to retain their rights and privileges because young people in poverty stay home from school, cut class, ignore assignments, and defy authority. Without their defiance, the fuel for the education wars would burn out. Insurgent slaves would not tolerate political arrangements that left them enslaved, and eventually forced those arrangements to change. Similarly, young people today—whether recognized as political agents or not—defy educational arrangements that lock them into second-class citizenship; they are pushing and will continue to push on those educational arrangements until the whole country is forced to confront and change the caste system of education.

It might be objected that slaves were escaping from conditions that were detrimental to their well-being in every conceivable way, but the education that young people resist today is at least potentially helpful to them,

and certainly the extent of physical and emotional oppression that they suffer is incomparable to slavery.
Maybe so, although not everyone would agree that even
"successful" state education has a benign effect. Our
point, however, is not that the conditions young people
oppose in schools are equivalent to the conditions slaves
opposed. We are saying only that the fact of young people's resistance to schooling and the fact of slaves running away and seeking to free themselves both have and
had the parallel political effect of white people coming
into conflict *with each other* in reaction to the slaves' and
their descendants' actions.

Still, it is hard to ignore the obvious parallels between the plantation owners' analysis of slave behavior
and the typical theories and systems of control employed
by most twenty-first century schools for young people
in poverty. Both systems rely on coercion, because they
interpret the slaves' or students' motives as either bes-
tial or diseased. For example: "In working niggers, we
always calculate that they will not labor at all except to
avoid punishment, and they will never do more than just
enough to save themselves from being punished, and
no amount of punishment will prevent their working
carelessly or indifferently."[6] The same theories in almost
the same words can be heard in many staff lounges,
and not only from white teachers. The punishments
envisioned are various humiliations along the lines of
course failure and "being written up" as first steps to-

6   Frederick Law Olmstead, *A Journey to the Seaboard Slave
States* (New York, 1863), 210. Cited in "Day to Day Resis-
tance to Slavery," *Journal of Negro History*, vol. 27 (1942),
which is reprinted in *Rebellions, Resistance, and Runaways
Within the Slave South*, ed. Paul Finkelman (New York and
London: Garland Publishing, 1989), 84–116.

ward physical exclusion from the class or school. Not
only informal attitudes, but the official policies of most
schools for adolescents in poverty assume that without
"consequences" (the twentieth-century euphemism for
"punishment"), students would do no academic work at
all, probably would not even bother attending school or
classes, and would, most likely, run amok. A whole pan-
oply of physical movements are alternately prescribed
and proscribed: where the students must or may not
sit; where they must or may not go; which doors they
are required and which doors they are forbidden to use;
which books or materials they must or may not touch;
which websites they may see or must not see; when they
must stand and when they may not stand; when they
may use the bathroom; when they may eat; when they
may or must leave the building; when they may or must
speak. All these modal constraints depend utterly on
punishment and the threat of punishment. Well-run
schools, like well-run plantations, are places where the
"consequences" for violating requirements are swift and
certain. And for most teachers, administrators, students,
and parents, it is unthinkable that students would go
where they are "supposed to," "do their work," or "stop
talking" unless they feared punishment—humiliation,
failure, or physical exclusion. Plantations developed
elaborate pass systems to control the movements of
slaves, and schools for children in poverty often require
all students outside of class to carry a pass issued by a
teacher or authority. Slaveholders developed systems of
patrol to prevent unauthorized movements and to return slaves to the plantations. Schools for students in
poverty hire police, security officers, and "hall monitors"
to patrol inside schools, demanding to see passes, and

police daily arrive at schools with vanloads of truant students who have been apprehended for existing where they do not belong. Places of detention and humiliation, stocks and stockades, were established to confine difficult, unruly slaves. Schools for poor children have "in-school suspension" centers where disobedient students must sit all day, often forbidden to speak. The official, written policy in the school where I teach commands that students on "in-school suspension" must sit facing the wall, each young person forbidden to look at any other. The policy does not yet require students to be placed in physical stocks.

As in the slave system, each attempt by powerful authorities to seal a crack through which the desire for life and action leaks out is answered by a new escape, a new breakout, a new assertion of purposes and intentions distinct from the authorities'. And in an unbroken cycle, the powerful authorities find themselves constrained to move again, to move in reaction to those they thought weaker, usually trying again to seal up life, only rarely acceding to the other's intentions, only rarely opening up a way for more life.

What role do young people in poverty play today in the political life of the country, of cities, suburbs, and rural areas, of communities, and particularly, of schools? By "political" we mean: having to do with the life of the polis or republic; in one's role as a citizen; contributing to the ordering of social relations; affecting who has power to do what.

"A fully moral act is basically an act *now*. It is not promissory, it is not 'investing for future profit.' It is not the learning of a technique in the hopes this technique, when learned, will enable one to make wheels [turn] ....

A fully moral act is a total assertion at the time of the assertion. Among other things it has a *style*—and this style is an integral aspect of its meaning."[7]

The roles of young people in relation to schools and communities are often shaped as a series of "fully moral acts," and can be distinguished from their assigned technocratic roles, just as total assertions in the present moment can be distinguished from promissory notes or investments, that is, from reductions of complex relationships, strategies, and interactions to simplistic "bottom lines," or "data trends." Young people do not react to behavioral stimuli as dogs do. They act, and they act in their powerful capacity as human beings, which means that they compel re-actions in other human beings, whether those others like the interaction or not.

The disruptive student effectively derails a teacher's carefully planned lesson and inaugurates a whole series of disciplinary, behavioral, and professional "interventions." Classes of middle schoolers often boast that they made this teacher quit or that teacher cry, and the principal's evaluation is affected in many ways by such factors as teachers quitting because of student behavior. Gang members' violent behavior shakes out tens or hundreds of thousands of dollars in billable hours for ambulance drivers, police, lawyers, judges, probation officers, social workers, lab assistants, jailers, and all their bureaucratic superiors. These young people are not thinking of "consequences." They are acting *now*, and with style.

Burke's word "style" might seem odd here; but it is meant to call attention to the difference between the graceless, literal, pseudo-scientific diction of the lesson

---

7   Kenneth Burke, *The Philosophy of Literary Form* (Berkeley: University of California, 1973/1941), 148.

plan or social work protocol, the stiffness in the posture of the young, partially trained teacher at the whiteboard, on the one hand, and on the other hand the scowling, muscular throwing over of the desk by the angry student. Human acts are layered with symbolic meanings that represent complex strategies for coping with life's troubles and opportunities. Descriptions of human acts that try to eliminate those symbolic meanings, echoes, implicit identifications, and strategies are inaccurate descriptions.

In a different way, students act now and with style who commit their whole being to the school play, or to the poems they are writing, or to their competition for an A in math. These ways of acting may be more "useful" in the long run or more profitable to the students than disrupting class or stabbing a peer, but it is generally accurate to describe both the pro-social and the antisocial acts of young people as serving their interests in the moment. The thrill of the drama; the power of the developing voice and body; the mother's or father's or gang leader's approval evoking home and safety; the chemistry of the dance: these things get more accurately at the motives of most adolescents than citing their regard for college applications, test scores, or job resumes. Accurate descriptions of motives show common ground between youth called "model" and youth called "delinquent." Their acts fit present purposes in ways that feel right to them stylistically at the moment of action.

In contrast, "evidence-based," technocratic descriptions of student "behaviors" focus on stimulus and response. Does stimulus A result in response B? We are not very bothered if the response we are asked to produce changes from B to C to D. The technocrat does not judge the value or style of the indicated responses, and asks only that the young people and their teachers accept them as given. The technocrat's job is simply to find the correct stimulus for producing whatever response is required—whatever response is required in whatever target the technocrats have identified for their "intervention."

In the normal technocratic view, we do not distinguish the variety of motives that might point a community of people toward a given purpose. The question of purpose, from this point of view, must be settled in advance; nowadays, these are almost always elaborate lists of standards, goals, objectives, indicators, and so on, pompously "scientific" in style. Young people play no official role at all in the creation of these lists. The lists, rather, are intended to operate as definitive of the young people's status vis-à-vis whatever institution the lists govern. In the technocrat's ideal school, for example, the significant "behaviors" of students are intended to be predictable responses to carefully chosen stimuli designed to result over time in the brain-states leading to the correct bubbles being filled in on the required tests. But these purported institutional purposes of the state, the lists of what students "should know and be able to do," are obviously inaccurate descriptions of the young people's purposes. The restricted role implied for students—to exhibit the "behaviors" that satisfy institutional purposes— are obviously different from the roles the young people are constructing for themselves. Neutrality of persons; neutrality of purposes; neutrality of means on the one hand versus the fully moral acts of young people making "total assertions at the time of the assertion" on the other.

On some level of generality, adolescents cannot be certain of purposes in advance of their action. They try on personas, adjust them, fit them to new purposes and

scenes and discover new ways of acting as a greater reper-
toire of means develops in their minds and bodies. Experimenting with a hair style or a way of dancing or deciding
to hang out in a certain teacher's room or at a rec center or
on a corner are actions that may lead to new purposes, unpredictable or even unimaginable before the experiment
begins. In this sense, actions shape character and purpose
as much as character and purpose shape action.

Imagining that the purposes of schools are settled is a
way of hiding the political role of young people. Imagining that what remains to do is simply the implementation
of proven technologies for the production of accepted
social purposes misrepresents the sociological and political problem. The problem is that the social and political
purposes of the country are contested, and young people
are already participating in working toward a settlement
of the contest, even while their political role remains
unacknowledged. Their participation compels reactions
from all parties just as an entrance or an outburst by a
character on stage compels reactions from other characters or from the audience.

The shifting, inconstant eruptions of young people's energy in schools and communities never quiets
completely. As insistently and naïvely as infants do, but
layered with intricate abilities and new awareness, adolescents demand attention. But the young are rarely interpreted as fully human actors. More frequently, young
people are observed and analyzed as part of the scenic
background for the authorities' actions, as props or man-
nequins, objects upon which older people deploy their
stimuli to produce the "mandated" responses.

This increasingly standardized official frame for
viewing the acts of young people is awkward, both

historically and in light of our actual human relations. The frame contrives to position complete human beings as admittedly intricate, but predictable automata. Automata have no moral dimension or role. They simply behave as programmed. But the ordinary, daily practice of every culture has been to worry constantly over the moral and social development of children and adolescents. In the past, pubescent youth did well or badly because they were obedient or diligent or brave or lazy or cowardly or willful or depraved or wicked or good. And, of course, even in our era of very strange namings, everyone in actual relationship with young people interprets what youth do using moral categories, among others. We are constantly exhorting the young to act this way or that way, but we would never dream of using exhortation on a machine.[8]

The contrast is extreme between what are now called "scientific" practices in schools and the ordinary moral categories teachers and parents habitually use. Teachers are now ordered to perform "functional behavioral assessments" on students who are disruptive or insubordinate. These are flow charts, like engineering diagrams, that the behaviorists assure us can be used to adjust inputs and environmental variables until the intended "output" is produced. Devised by "scientists" at the Johns Hopkins University, the protocols inform teachers that they are only to consider what takes place "three minutes to three seconds before and three seconds to three minutes after" the behavior that is scheduled to be "extinguished" occurs.[9]

---

8 Burke, *A Grammar of Motives*, 59–60.
9 Instructions given at a mandatory professional development session for teachers conducted by Baltimore City Public Schools, September, 2011.

Even with a functional behavioral assessment in hand, however, teachers and parents ubiquitously discuss the morality of students' actions: "They know right from wrong. They are stubborn or obstinate; they are trying to 'get over' or to get away with bad behavior. They are lazy or disrespectful. They are traveling with the wrong crowd. They should try harder. They are choosing not to try or are choosing to disrupt." Or even, "Their parents are lazy, obstinate, ignorant, and allow their children too much freedom." These things may all be said with venom or with love, with subtlety or coarsely. They may contribute in the total context to an accurate and helpful or to an inaccurate and unhelpful "summing up" of the complete situation. The point is not that every description using moral categories is correct and every description using "scientific" categories is incorrect, but rather that complete descriptions of human acts include moral terms, and that overemphasis on one set of terms or another is bound to weaken the description.

It cannot be accurate and precise to interpret a teenager's behavior as simply mechanical, as nothing more than the response to external stimuli. Although there are many things we can predict about what other people might do, there are also many things we hope for or fear but that remain unpredictable, things that we can literally know only "in the event" or after the fact. Similarly, other people may make many correct predictions about what we ourselves will do; but their predictions never deprive us of the experience of consciousness, our absolute certainty that much of what we do is a result of our intentions, choices, purposes, or will, and is not forced on us by anything pre-ordained or ordered before our decision to act.

The authorities' current obsession with "evaluating teacher performance" is best analyzed in these terms: from the technocratic point of view, no matter which students are enrolled in a class and no matter what those students choose to do, their teachers should be able to employ the appropriate stimuli for creating the state-mandated response. The "teacher performance" obsession has room for only one fully human actor, the teacher, because the "reformers" postulate that nothing the students do can possibly undermine the highly skilled teacher's intentions. "Students of good teachers will learn" is taken by technocratic education reformers as a scientifically true statement—a literal correspondence to reality—not much different in status from "UPS procedures result in on-time delivery of parcels," or "Bridges built to code will bear X volume of traffic for Y years." The fact that the teachers' procedures operate on persons—fully moral actors in their own right, who may have procedures, intentions, and actions of their own to contribute to the playing out of the drama—is a fact absent from the current policy dicta.

Technocratic confidence, at least in public, knows no bounds. The remarkable No Child Left Behind Act of 2001 actually predicted its version of educational perfection by 2014: All American children and adolescents would be literate and numerate as measured on standardized tests by that date. The most deceptive aspect of this prediction is not that the goal might be "unattainable." Rather, what is most deceptive is that the goal has little to do with the education of human children, that is, nothing to do with the purposes the children and adolescents might themselves have. If the evaluation were integrated into the actual purposes of children's lives, it might be possible for teachers and students to collaborate toward creating a world that meets their needs. But to bubble in an answer cannot be a moral act; it is no kind of assertion at all, let alone a total assertion in the moment. It is merely something a person might do who is temporarily ceding, for whatever reason, their personhood to someone else's control. The reduction of education to "measureable" test scores, and the constant boasting about or castigation of this or that set of scores by various authorities and researchers is only hubris— the pretense that the human subjects of these tests are as manipulable and susceptible to arbitrary adjustment as automata. This point is far from subtle and can hardly be disputed. A test result might tell us something about what a student knows. Teachers affect what students know. But how could we conclude from these premises that teachers *cause* test results? At the very least we would have to say that the teacher *and the student* together cause the test result. That's why we praise both of them when they do well.

That the authorities' pronouncements tend toward the exaltation of the puppeteers' powers at the expense of the puppets' should come as no surprise. To the extent that young people's actions can be reduced rhetorically to "behaviors" susceptible to protocols of control, their political role is partially neutralized. What is more difficult to see is the way the authorities have adapted an old rhetorical strategy to the present times, while maintaining the fraudulent appeal to "science" as the core of their argument.

Earlier in the nation's history, many social scientists, psychologists, and public officials claimed that biological facts explained the laziness, stupidity, venality, or

criminality of certain groups of young people as compared to others. These explanations fit well with racist judgments about values—who was to be classed as
"good" or "advanced" and who was to be classed as "bad"
or "primitive." However, the partial successes of the freedom movement in the 1950s and 1960s made it difficult
to explain differences in levels of education by official or
overt appeals to these "scientific" facts about race. One
prominent strategy in response to this difficulty was to
situate "culture" rather than "race" as the scientific reality behind poverty and lack of education. This strategy
is still prominent, particularly in the version that blames
parents for their children's poor performance in school.

Of course, parents, communities, and cultures are
important terms in any complete description of how
children grow up to be adults. We are saying only that
the *reduction* of a young person's development to nothing
more than the result of parenting or the social environment is necessarily incomplete, and leads to inaccurate
descriptions, especially when the descriptions of family
and culture are themselves thin reductions. Children of
the same parents and of the same social environment do
not grow up to be "the same." An accurate, truly scientific
description must include qualities of the young people
and their families as actors in their own right, must include impulses and motives deriving from *their* purposes,
not just the authorities', and must include a full appreciation of their individual and collective action that is never
still, always shifting, and always eliciting reactions and
responses, leading to new stances and new actions.

More recently, attacks on "parents" and "culture"
have also been challenged as racist, and authorities have
therefore discovered teachers to be the new scapegoats

of "science." The argument starts from the premise that "disadvantaged" people are entirely correct in saying that there is nothing wrong with their children or their culture. This premise is encapsulated in the slogan, "All children can learn." If all children *can* learn, but only some children *do* learn, the technocrats postulate a cause for learning or lack of learning that can neither reside in the child, which would be racist, nor in the family or culture, which would also be racist, and so must reside—according to this theory—in the teacher. Now the facts (1) that this explanation has come about at a time of high unemployment among young white college graduates and (2) that the majority of teachers who are classified by the technocrats' "scientific measures" as inadequate are teachers of color, have not yet registered in the "reformers'" eyes as racist. Our point here, however, is only that the authorities' justification for their claim that these teachers are good while those teachers are bad is based on "scientific data," just as were the earlier claims about intellectual or moral differences between the races, or about social "pathologies."

Teachers and the culture of the family are thus the principal factors now held responsible in the official debate about young people's learning or failing to learn. Certainly, these factors are important, and for younger children they may dominate. But children, as they enter adolescence, have something of their own to say about the formation of their intellectual and social attributes; they have power to act in what they believe are their own interests, and they do.

If students in urban and poor rural high schools did what they were told, there would be no crisis in education. The thousands and thousands of attempts to reform individual secondary schools and the perennial systemic initiatives would be successful, except that young people don't cooperate, by and large, with the attempts. What are called failing schools are not places where the students attend regularly, listen to the teachers, complete assignments and homework, but fail to learn anyway. They are schools where the students evade or defy authority's demands: they stay home, roam the halls, don't listen, neglect homework, and act out. Reflexively today, public policies say adults are accountable for this non-compliance and that if either the teachers or the parents or both did their jobs properly, the students would learn, which effectively means "would comply." The possibility should be considered, however, that young people evade adult demands not because adults are inexpert in framing those demands, not because adults have yet to find the correct rewards, punishments, resources, environments, and curricula to secure compliance, but rather because the young people have different purposes and different interests from the adults, and are pursuing those purposes and interests according to their own plans, often successfully.

Although we adults tend to think about this subject in terms of adolescents either doing what they are told or defying authority, many adolescents think less abstractly. Not paying much attention to the rules or demands of authorities, they try to meet someone they want to meet, or they look for news about what interests them, or spend time with a friend, or experiment with their bodies, or listen to music, watch a video, sleep, eat, read or write (but not the reading or writing teachers assign), and so on. The fact that adults at school and often at home are making demands on them is not at the center of their thinking, but may rather be only a minor or major irritation depending on the specific demand and on the severity of the adults' response to noncompliance. And in order to pursue their own purposes, young people may develop more or less complex strategies of avoiding and resisting authority. Often the young people's techniques of avoidance and resistance are successful. They succeed in hearing the gossip, or having sex, or taking or selling drugs, or playing football when they should be in class, or composing a poem or a piece of music, or leaving school to eat a meal. Parents and teachers who feel enlightened appreciate that young people have their own perception of needs and desires and try to persuade them that there are ways to satisfy those needs and desires while still complying with adult demands. It may be true that the tiny number of relatively successful secondary schools for young people in poverty have quite a large overlap between the activities that satisfy the young people and those that count as satisfying the older people, too. But the great majority of young people in poverty are not persuaded that their needs and desires can be met at the same time as they satisfy adults' demands, and the great majority of adults are not persuaded either. On the contrary, the common, shared view about poor and working-class youth tends to be that compliance with adult demands requires coercion on the part of adults and sacrifice—what we often call "postponement of gratification"—on the part of the young. To the extent that young people do not accept this sacrifice of what they perceive to be in their own interest, the plans and programs of the adults collapse.

The individual person, striving to form himself in accordance with the communicative norms that match the cooperative ways of his society, is by the same token concerned with the rhetoric of identification. To act upon himself persuasively, he must variously resort to images and ideas that are formative. Education ("indoctrination") exerts such pressure upon him from without; he completes the process from within. If he does not somehow act to tell himself (as his own audience) what the various brands of rhetoric have told him, his persuasion is not complete. Only those voices from without are effective which can speak in the language of a voice within.[10]

This is not simply a question of "understanding the student's culture" or of listening to their music or being familiar with their neighborhoods—approaches often suggested in colleges of education. Of course, these things are potentially useful, but they are still external to the "language of the voice within." That most intimate language and voice is the one the students use when they are talking to themselves, inside of and building their own consciousness, when they exhort and persuade themselves as their own audience, seeking to identify their true interests and to put themselves in motion in service to those interests. Burke's insight into education is that the interior dialogue must somehow match and complement the socialization attempted by teachers, parents, and authorities ("socialization as a moralizing process"). Educational psychologists talk about the importance of "internalization" of concepts, or about "metacognition." These terms are intended to name developments in students that are related to Burke's idea, but he is looking at the students from a

---

10 Burke, *A Rhetoric of Motives*, 39.

different perspective. To him, young people do not wait to be educated before they begin to hear the voices of authority in their heads; by virtue of their humanity they are *already* "striving to form [themselves] in accordance with the communicative norms that match the cooperative ways of [their] society." They are already "acting upon [themselves] persuasively" and at any given time in their lives have already internalized reams of both explicit and more subtle strategies and tactics from their elders. The question cannot simply be how the teacher's voice—through "instruction," repetition, and carefully designed experiences—can become a voice the students will hear inside their own minds in the teacher's absence. The prior, more fundamental question is how that internalized voice either becomes a part of or remains separate from the student's interior dialogue, the rhetorical effort addressed to themselves that the young people are already engaged in *for their own purposes.*

Pragmatically, Burke's insight explains the strange absence of intellectual engagement in most high schools. The curriculum speaks in a language that is almost impossible for students in poverty to attend to, let alone incorporate into their interior dialogue as a way of completing the process of socialization. The issue is not only the difference in "content" between the students' concerns and the official concerns. It is that the "cooperative norms and communicative ways" of the official institution are not the "cooperative norms and communicative ways" that the students are striving to form themselves in accordance with. They are indeed striving to be socialized because they are alive and human, but they are striving to be socialized into the actual ways poor people in America survive—surviving, that is, in a society that is not arranged to meet their needs and that is full of absurdity, of senseless obstacles to life. The official curriculum, in contrast, represents the idealized socialization of the middle-class suburb, illusions and all, where human needs are presumed to be met, and where arrangements for material needs, at least, make more sense.

Seventy-five percent of the country's schools function relatively well by international testing standards. If the lowest-performing quartile is excluded from comparisons, US schools perform about as well as Singapore's, often held up as exemplary on international scales.[11] In these relatively successful schools (a category correlated very closely with higher socio-economic status), parents, teachers, and administrators can make plans with some confidence that students will mostly collaborate. It is an untested question whether the students would continue to collaborate if they were deprived of the perquisites of affluence: their cars and their parents' cars, their phones, their computers, their music, their well-equipped school facilities, their well-stocked refrigerators and cafeterias, their lavish sports programs, bands, dances, allowances, summer camps, internships, and so on. As things stand, these affluent students mostly go with the program, incorporating the socializing rhetoric from without into their interior dialogue.

In the bottom quartile, "low-performing" schools, however (which overwhelmingly means schools for the poor and working-class), young people effectively prevent the smooth implementation of plans and policies

---

11 Organisation for Economic Co-operation and Development (OECD), *Programme for International Student Assessments* (2009). http://www.oecd.org/pisa/pisaproducts/pisa2009keyfindings.htm.

no matter what their teachers or parents do. An adolescent who chooses not to go to school or not to read an assignment, not to write an essay or perform an experiment or answer a question or work with a group, cannot be compelled. When hundreds or thousands of students choose to ignore a school's program or participate only in trivial and superficial ways, the schools are said to fail. To prevent the appearance of failure, schools often change what they ask students to do until their requests match the trivial level of participation that the students accede to. Schools or teachers that insist on what are called "higher standards" quickly find themselves accused of failing too many students, of not "meeting the students where they are," or of skimming off only the compliant students. Even the schools that exercise authority to exclude noncompliant students often find themselves vulnerable to the young people's power; many students understand that schools can only afford to exclude the worst offenders. "As long as I am not the worst, I am safe," goes the thinking, and "standards" drop accordingly.

There are certainly examples of teachers and some small schools whose working-class students are, on average, much more deeply involved in learning than is typical. And there are plenty of examples where individual students and teachers develop deep and intense intellectual conversations that benefit both teacher and learner. These things are possible, but far from routine. The ordinary exchange in schools and classrooms for adolescents in poverty is the regular adult contortion to produce compliance and the students' apparently supercilious choosing to comply or not comply with official procedures as they go about their other affairs.

Supercilious, but also tortured, because despite their openly aggressive or passively aggressive responses to authority, young people in poverty become aware of the society's essential neglect or open fear of them as they move through adolescence. Their analyses of their social roles are frequently deep, and the surfaces they present often disguise complex thinking and subtle understanding of the double-bind they are in: there is no way out of poverty except through school, but high poverty schools inspire little confidence that even compliance will be rewarded with economic security (and, in fact, the data support the increasing elusiveness of economic security for all but the wealthy). Furthermore, the interests of the school—the obsession with test scores, the inflexibility of schedules deliberately designed to thwart "socializing," the constant presence of police and guards, the insistence on the unconditional authority of teachers and administrators—are almost impossible to reconcile with the immediate needs of adolescents. Young people know intuitively that they must figure out how to become adults, but that their schools are designed to infantilize them, to simplify and standardize their verbal expression, to restrict and control their bodies, to crush independent, nonconforming thought. Nevertheless, nearly everyone they trust tells them school is the only way out of poverty and dependency.

The academic analysis of youth of color's defiance of authority and resistance to "acting white" is relevant here, but generally misses the point. This debate has centered on the question of whether youth of color and particularly black youth choose not to do well in school because doing well in school is derided by their peers as "acting white." Research has been inconclusive

on that question,[12] but a correct analysis would clari-
fy that "doing well in school" can mean two different
things in accordance with the two distinct functions of
education. "Doing well in school" can mean "learning,"
or it can mean "accepting socialization in conformity
to authority's demands." Adults and especially education authorities conflate the two functions, but young
people are often clear on the difference. All young people and all youth cultures respect and seek knowledge
and learning. Young people of all cultures are ashamed
when they appear ignorant and proud when they know
things. What young people may deride, however, is the
appearance of siding with authority in the school project of enforcing obedience; or the appearance of siding
with white society in maintaining the normative values
and power that keep descendants of slaves oppressed.
Carrying a book or completing an assignment can
sometimes signal conformity to normative values, but
students are neither proud to be ignorant nor disparaging of peers' knowledge; they are proud to be defiant,
and disparaging of sycophancy and group betrayal.

Young people in their own places away from adult
authority discuss, debate, and explore all kinds of things:
they know and respect when someone is smart, quick,
skilled, experienced, and well-informed. They take offense not at a peer's knowledge or intelligence, but at
a peer's rejection of the shared culture that necessarily
has aspects of resistance built in. A young person may be
popular and still read a lot, but the reading is often not

---

12 Roland G. Freyer and Paul Torelli, "An Empirical Analysis
of 'Acting White.'" National Bureau of Economic Research
Working Papers Series, May 2005. http://www.nber.org/
papers/w11334.pdf.

what the teachers assign. A student may get very good grades and still be well-liked, but only if they spend time maintaining relationships through common interests and adventures, and pursue friendships with students whose grades are worse. And a whole group of friends can define themselves as good at school but also "conscious," which means "aware of and resistant to oppression." Because passively accepting an inferior caste status is problematic to youth in poverty, the authorities' conflation of obedience with learning reinforces resistance to school. It would be better to distinguish these two functions of education—acquiring knowledge vs. accepting socialization into an unjust society. Young people want to learn; but they don't want to be stepped on. They are able to distinguish their own interests from the interests of the school, and they act accordingly.

When we understand that young people are often effective in developing and advancing their plans and projects autonomously, the mammoth failure of school reform makes more sense. Just as runaway slaves undermined the institutions of slavery, young people are able to derail educational reforms simply by acting in what they believe are their interests. Generally, in the behavior modification mode of treating young people as if they were circus animals, reforms are conceived as either carrots or sticks. The sticks include bad grades, high-stakes tests, "consequences" for poor attendance or poor performance, grade retention, suspension, expulsion, and even incarceration. In theory, facing these grave consequences, the students should choose to do as they are told. But a very large number of young people in each generation for fifty years have reacted with boredom or anger, rather than with awe, to the authorities' threats. Rather than enforce obedience, the consequences either chase students away from particular schools or from school altogether, or it sets students in motion to find the surface behavior that passes for the desired behavior and so evades punishment. Millions of students who are coerced into attending school seal up their emotions, spirit, and intellect during class, offering a passive bodily presence that counts as attendance, but that involves virtually no intellectual or emotional engagement and no learning at all. Tens of thousands of students cope with this coercion every day by attending school drunk or high or plugged constantly into music, literally anesthetizing themselves to avoid the pain of being separated from what they need to live. For many, many students the threat of failing a course or a grade is almost meaningless. Authorities intend for the students to reason that effort will pay off, but the students choose instead to take their chances on pursuing their own interests and purposes. The subsequent failure—if it occurs—is just one more in a long list of arbitrary ills that afflict most working-class Americans. The threat of failing a course is only intimidating if students believe they are losing something important; when the rest of their lives convinces them that they are likely to lose most of what they care about anyway, course failure is hardly a threat.

Many teachers and parents argue that the ineffectiveness of these stick-like consequences derives from the inconsistency with which they are applied. This may be true to some extent. The point here is not that the sticks are necessarily or theoretically ineffective, but rather that in the actual circumstances of contemporary American schools, students respond to the threats and punishments in ways that reformers do not intend and that pragmatically undermine the reforms.

An outstanding case study is the high-stakes examinations in Maryland. When half the students in the state and seventy percent of poor students were failing the trial versions of these tests, the state superintendent explained that the scores reflected the students' awareness that the trial tests "didn't count," that is "had no punitive consequence"; she predicted the scores would go up once the tests were actually required for graduation. When the tests were given in earnest and counted toward graduation, unacceptably large percentages of students, mostly poor and African American, still failed. To cope with the unacceptable failure rate, the state school board instituted an alternative procedure that would substitute for passing the tests; with guidance from a teacher, students could complete a series of prescribed booklets containing relevant questions and problems in each subject area. Schools now scramble to complete and submit thousands of these booklets each year for evaluation as test substitutes; often, teachers more or less dictate the answers to the students. Often the students take the booklets home and have a friend or relative complete them. The stick of failing the high-stakes test and so not graduating was, it seems, not brutal enough to obtain submission from the students and so rather than learn more, the failing students have effectively manipulated teachers and administrators into "co-constructing" the illusion of learning. Even so, another large subset still simply leaves school without passing either the tests or the alternatives in any form. It is doubtful whether the institution of high stakes testing has increased learning very much. SAT scores have been flat in the five years since the tests counted for graduation. In any case, no testing regimen ever deprives adolescents of their capacity to resist testing.

The carrots are of many different kinds. Less seriously, schools use pizza, trips to amusement parks, and
homework passes. More seriously, they develop curricula
and behavior management techniques that acknowledge
students' interests, curiosity, and humanity to varying de-
grees. On top of this relatively humanistic approach, a few
innovators understand that poverty does not make learning impossible, but complicates it tremendously. These
few innovators try to substitute "services" for the absence
of viable material conditions in impoverished neighborhoods: health care, counseling, drug treatment, recreation,
internships, and so on. Many young people appreciate
these services and take advantage of them to an extent,
but the programs offered are far from comprehensive and
we have enough experience with social services to know
that services cannot replace a viable society. Nevertheless,
the point again is that if either a carrot or a stick works to
increase young people's learning, it is because the young
people understand the carrot or stick as advancing their
own interests and meeting their needs. They may act with
passive aggression, but they are not passive. Their behavior may be treated as the mechanical output of various
technocratic inputs, but there will remain a substantial
and often determining remainder of motivation that
derives not from the teachers', schools' or parents' con-
trivances, but from the young people's thoughts, beliefs,
emotions, physical need, desires, intentions, and ways of
coping with the difficulties of their lives.

The specific ways young people interrupt or undo reformers' plans can be described with some precision. They
can (1) refuse to comply with the teachers' and school's
demands or (2) comply, but only superficially, and so still
learn little or nothing. There are nearly infinite examples.

Obviously, students must be in school and in class for the teacher's technique to matter at all. So the first way students can interrupt "reforms" is by not coming to school. But even if they are in school and in class, and even if the lesson is magnificent, the student must choose to engage with the curriculum, to think about the questions asked, to make an attempt at answering questions, to write what they may be asked to write or measure what they are asked to measure or to come up with questions of their own. Curriculum is usually prescribed today as a sequence and script, or lesson plans that are close in style to a script. Things like:

- "Ask the students what they see under the microscopes. Answers will vary, but may include 'wiggly things,' 'There are little black dots…', etc."
- "Ask the students to draw what they see."

The controlling theory of these curricula is that what happens in the students' brains because of the scripted interactions will cause the students to choose correct answers on the standardized tests. But a student may simply operate from a different script. For example, instead of describing what they see under the microscope, they raise their hand and when called on ask to go to the bathroom. Or, rather than listening to or hearing the instruction to describe what they see under the microscope, they are listening to music, or to a friend, or texting, or are thinking about how hungry they are, or what to say to a girl or boy that they like, or are worrying about money, or their clothes, or any of a thousand other things.. Or the students may simply put their heads down and sleep. A "better" teacher who may be more engaging, may love the subject matter more, may be funnier, may be more in tune with the students' culture, may be better liked by the students or more patient or creative in rephrasing the script, or more expert in maintaining order and focus, may also get a higher proportion of students to respond as prescribed and this may result in the students choosing correct answers on the standardized tests more frequently. Nevertheless, the students are not automata and are able to act in ways not prescribed by the curriculum, and often *do* act in ways not prescribed, even when their teachers are skilled enough to implement the curriculum appropriately.

The data, in any event, are very clear: no matter how skilled the teachers, they cannot consistently produce desired "learning behavior" in young adults whom the society has relegated to "bottom quartile," secondary schools. The most sophisticated statistical models are still unable reliably to correlate "effective teachers" with student learning—even measured by the questionable criteria of test scores. Teachers who are rated as "most effective" with one class can be rated as "least effective" with another class in the very same year.[13] It is strange, but this fact sends the psychometricians on a quest for better quantitative analysis in an attempt to identify the "good" teachers. A more rational response would be to acknowledge that there is at least one other category of agent involved in the development of students' brains, namely, the students.

Another way the students can undermine curricular reform is to act in the prescribed ways, but only

13 Linda Darling-Hammond et al, *Getting Teacher Evaluation Right: A Background Paper for Policymakers* (American Educational Research Association 2011), http://www.aera.net/Portals/38/docs/About_AERA/GettingTeacher EvaluationRightBackgroundPaper(1).pdf.

superficially and formally, without engaging in the cognitive back and forth that would result in real learning.
The better the curriculum, the harder it is to avoid that
deeper cognitive interaction; but the deeper the cognitive
interaction demanded in the curriculum, the less pre-
scriptive it becomes about the teacher and student roles.
Regardless of whether one curriculum is better or worse
than another, to the extent that students engage only superficially—outwardly obedient, inwardly distracted or
"just getting it over with," or copying from a friend—the
learning intended by the reform is unlikely to occur.

Various reforms respond more or less directly to this
aspect of actual student control. For example: The Co-
alition of Essential Schools developed an approach to
reduce superficial student interactions and to increase
student engagement with material. This is also a goal
of the National Council of Teachers of Mathematics's
stress on creative problem solving as opposed to teaching
repetitive algorithms. It is also a goal of the new Common Core mathematics guidelines that are part of the
movement for national standards. However, if these in-
novations result in more learning, the cause will be not
only the acts of teachers and parents, but also the acts of
students in pursuit of their own purposes.

On the other side of the coin, certain curricula include
detailed behavior management techniques to reduce the
instances when students veer from the prescribed script
or lesson. Examples of this are certain practices in KIPP
schools and MATCH schools, the kind of schools that
are influential in the expansion of charters and that contribute to the fueling of the charter debate. In addition,
there is an entire, and very large, industry of behavior
management coaching and professional development

that tries to regulate student responses so they will fit as much of the curricular script as possible.

It seems beyond debate that the acts of noncompliant or disengaged students have given rise to these reform initiatives: Young people in poverty pursuing their own interests consistently undermine the smooth functioning of the schools they attend. The KIPP, MATCH, behavior management style of reform grows out of the view that particular techniques will result in the young people collaborating with the institutional interests of the school, deferring or subordinating any of their own interests that are institutionally incompatible. The reformers' theory says that skilled teachers can cope with any configuration at all of student "needs" and adjust their technique to compensate in whatever direction and to whatever extent required, as if they were champion archers who hit the bull's-eye every time in any wind or weather. The important observation is that these reforms imagine the intentions, desires, and actions of the students to be entirely subordinate to the teacher's intentions, desires, and actions. It is as if the students' independent interests were a disease that this style of reform is specifically designed to cure.

In the same way that the colonial power imagines the colony as "uninhabited," so the education reformers imagine the students as being without volition of their own, or at least without an autonomous volition. The colonist/educator believes that the colonized/student can be made to perform any action intended by the authorities. In contrast, an African-centered, anticolonial perspective specifically targets the cruelty of the colonizer, insisting: we are free, we can choose something else, you cannot explain our volition away. But the reformers have learned less than nothing from Paolo Freire half a century after take too much initiative and willfully propel themselves in all kinds of directions not determined by the lesson plan. They talk to each other about their own affairs, or they plan somewhere to go besides to school. They introduce themselves to new people, arrange a game of basketball or a party or a gang fight or an economic or sexual transaction of some kind. Far from being passive, they are much too active and exhibit remarkable agency. The view that they are empty of agency or intentionality and that they must be taught to initiate activity is obviously absurd and comes from forgetting or denying that the students are alive, vital, without need of formal instruction to want, desire, and move. The words "motivated" and "unmotivated" have themselves been appropriated to imply values or direction aligned with institutional interests. To be motivated in school specifies an impulse to move toward good grades, diplomas, academic and eventually, economic success. Good teachers are said to motivate their students to learn, setting them in motion along the path laid out by the curriculum. But anyone who deals regularly with young people knows that they are dangerous and unpredictable, and unlikely to remain still and quiet. Leave them alone for a minute, and who knows what trouble they will get into. The problem of motivation is not that they don't move; the problem is that they don't move in the interests of others unless coerced. This is often called defiance, but many students going about their own business are perplexed when authorities charge them with defiance. "Defiance" in the authority's eyes seems to be what the students simply experience as "being alive."

Or ask it this way: Why are they defiant? Because there is actually no place for them. As Yolanda says wisely: "We throw pencils out the window because we *want* something." It is easy to see that the education system creates scarcity of knowledge by its nature: only some— not all—can be in the top classes and best schools, and it slowly dawns in adolescence how much or how little you will have access to. The sense of this scarcity is usually reinforced by the stances, acts, and words of adults, until the normal human urge to thrive, to live, the glory and energy of young people, pushes toward light and battles with whatever tries to cover or suppress them. "They are imbued with one fundamental certainty, that they have to destroy the continuously mounting bureaucratic mass, or themselves be destroyed by it."[14] They are trying to make room for themselves where there is no room yet. And the arguments of adults for this or that type of re- form—like the arguments earlier over fugitive slaves— are belated attempts to catch up with those who long ago initiated social and political transformations by their restless striving "to regain control over their conditions of life and their relations with one another."[15]

The current striving of young people, often disorga- nized, often entirely un-theorized, is a continuation of the struggle for freedom that has gone on for centuries before them. And just as in earlier times, young people still refuse to allow the powerful unlimited control, but will generate disorder whether they are recognized as human agents or not. Their fully moral acts cause reac- tions, willy-nilly. Those reactions include at least what we now name "education wars," and may even extend to many other political conflicts convulsing the nation in the twenty-first century.

---

14 C.L.R. James, Grace Lee Boggs, et al., *Facing Reality* (Chi- cago: Charles H. Kerr, 2006), 9.
15 Ibid., 9.

PART II

A Representative Anecdote: *Brown vs. Board* Taught in a Segregated Classroom

We will use Kenneth Burke's heuristic of a "representative anecdote" to develop a cluster of terms, images, and contexts that shed light on our analysis.[1] A representative anecdote contains the elements of scene, character, action, style, and purpose that operate on a societal level, but that let us tease out their relations in miniature.

The representative anecdote we have chosen is the act of teaching the Supreme Court decision *Brown vs. Board of Education* in a contemporary classroom for students in poverty, that is, in a segregated classroom. It might be helpful to imagine this classroom set up on a stage. Everyone on stage, except possibly the teacher, is black. Just beyond where the black students can see, a video is looping of another classroom, all white. Posters of Martin Luther King, Jr., Thurgood Marshall, and even Malcolm X, and photographs showing the Little Rock Nine entering Central High School hang on the classroom walls. On the white board, the teacher has just finished writing: "The Supreme Court decision of 1954, *Brown vs. Board,* ended segregation in American public schools."

---

1   Kenneth Burke, *A Grammar of Motives* (Berkeley: University of California, 1969/1945), 59.

Brown vs. Board is "mandated" curriculum across the country because it is a key chapter in the official narrative describing the nation's victory over racial discrimination, race prejudice, and inequality. But a pedagogical problem arises immediately. Segregated schools were declared unconstitutional in 1954, but here we are in 2014 sitting in a segregated classroom while we discuss implicitly the unlawfulness of our setting.

Looking more deeply, we notice that *Brown vs. Board* is taught as part of a chain of Supreme Court decisions: *Dred Scott, Plessy vs. Ferguson,* and *Brown.* The chain is taught as if it were a ladder rising toward freedom. Right at the bottom of the ladder, Chief Justice Taney in *Dred Scott* insisted that "the black man has no rights that a white man is bound to respect."[2] By the 1890s, slavery had ended, certain rights of black men, the story goes, were protected by the Civil War amendments, but a separation of the races was still held, in *Plessy,* to be prudent and constitutional. In 1954, however, the Court allowed the Constitution to shine forth in all its glory, complementing the end of slavery in 1865 with the end of segregation nearly a century later.

This limited series of Supreme Court decisions is unique in the standard high school history curriculum. With the possible exception of *Marbury vs. Madison,* no other Supreme Court cases are as widely or as regularly taught. The reason for the priority of these race-based decisions is that we Americans are a constitutional people, but the Constitution was flawed, and so we Americans needed a constitutional way to correct the flaw. From the perspective of most boards of education, that

---

2   *Dred Scott v. Sandford,* 60 U.S. 393 (The Supreme Court 1857).

constitutional way turns out to be the thirteenth, four-
teenth, and fifteenth amendments, *Brown vs. Board*, and
finally the Civil Rights and Voting Rights Acts of 1964
and 1965 to enforce the post-War amendments. The
Constitution as amended and interpreted has healed itself, according to this narrative. The stains spattered on
the founding document by slavery have been washed
away. And *Brown* is central to the purification because it
is held to have scrubbed off the effects of *Plessy* by elimi-
nating the doctrine of segregation from the crucial democratic institution of school.

This story is important to the curriculum because it is
a constitutional story. It dramatizes the foundation and
substance of the country: our goodness, our justice, our
equality, the rule of law, the founders' foresight in devising a mechanism for change, our self-sufficiency and
auto-correctibility—all grounded in the text of the Constitution, that impartial, superhuman, but humanly created instrument of the people. Without the "watershed"
of *Brown*, it would be hard to explain not only today's
legal protections against race discrimination, but also the
social opprobrium attaching in many milieus to explicit
racial stereotyping, slurs, and prejudices. Of course, the
story doesn't end with the 1954 decision. But descriptions of the Little Rock Nine or of James Meredith's
attempt to register at the University of Mississippi, for
example, make no sense unless *Brown vs. Board* is included as foreground. The Civil Rights Act of 1964, the
enormous increase in education funding for both white
children and children of color over the past fifty years,
the turmoil over forced busing and affirmative action, all
hinge on *Brown*. Its grandeur, the idealism of its vision,
the analysis of the centrality of education to democracy,

its insistence that equal protection and full citizenship require equality of educational opportunity have legitimated innumerable strategies and tactics over decades to advance the goals of equality. And those rippling effects of *Brown's* idealism, rooting desegregation explicitly in the Constitution, now soothe and assuage the national conscience as represented in the required curriculum of schools our children are compelled to attend. We do not discriminate. *Brown vs. Board* undid *Plessy vs. Ferguson*. *Plessy* asserted the constitutionality of segregation, but thereby dammed the nation's proper development. *Brown*, in reversing *Plessy*, swept away that constitutional dam and allowed the country's river of progress to flow, as it always should have, toward ever-increasing freedom and prosperity. The various boards of education, state and local, promote *Brown* as crucial evidence that the country is just, principled, and worthy of the students' allegiance. Officially, there is no embarrassment in celebrating *Brown's* respect for our children of color. Whatever the teacher, principal, or board member may actually feel about the relative qualities of the races, the inclusion of *Brown* in the curriculum allows and encourages them to say what they are expected to say: every student should be treated equally.

But the very grounding of *Brown's* conclusions in the bedrock of the Constitution, the drama of desegregation and equal protection of the laws, has allowed another drama to be detached from the official curriculum, a drama that has not yet found its way into a constitutional formulation except in the negative sense that the courts are not yet ready to touch it: that is, the drama of white flight and of black middle class escape, the resegregation of the schools and the hardening of the caste system in relation to our children. This other drama is rarely taught in schools nor "mandated" in most curricula. It is, however, the drama in which we Americans all are actors and that shapes our whole system of education, and many of the underlying currents in the republic's economic, social, and political development.

Many white families acted deliberately and thoughtfully to avoid sharing either their schools or their wealth with children of color. The historical process of that white flight has been widely documented by scholars and is hardly controversial. Key aspects of this history include enormous subsidies for highways and for gasoline, the mortgage interest deduction, and school construction funds, all to enable the rapid growth of white suburbs. But this recent history is mentioned only briefly in textbooks if it is mentioned at all, and "white flight" is left unanalyzed in schools as a continuation of the effects of *Plessy vs. Ferguson* through extra-judicial means.

We could imagine schools adding *San Antonio vs. Rodriquez* to the *Dred Scott, Plessy, Brown* series if the boards of education wanted to address white flight and the caste system more thoroughly. In *Rodriguez*, Mexican-American families attempted to dispute the constitutionality of wealthier white families choosing to keep their wealth for their own children's exclusive educational use.[3] The plaintiffs argued against the use of local property taxes as the main component of school funding by saying that the state could not support the establishment of school systems segregated de facto by the wealth of the residents. Lower state and federal courts agreed, holding that the intent of *Brown* was to prohibit not

---

3   *San Antonio v. Rodriguez*, 411 U.S. 1 (The Supreme Court 1973).

only laws that explicitly denied equal access to education, but also more subtle arrangements that led to the same de facto result. If the Supreme Court had upheld these lower court rulings in *Rodriguez*, it is conceivable that the great attraction of economically insulated school districts in the suburbs would have been much reduced. Wealthy suburbs and poor jurisdictions alike might have been compelled to fund school construction, teacher salaries, textbooks, technology, extracurricular programs and so on from one pooled state education budget on an equal footing, rather than from distinct district budgets with vast inequalities.

But the Supreme Court in *Rodriguez* ruled instead that there was no federal right to an education, and that the State of Texas could make whatever arrangements it chose in establishing a system of school financing, as long as those arrangements omitted *de jure* separation of rich and poor, or black, brown, and white.

With this constitutional assistance, the attraction of economically segregated suburban school districts grew rapidly until today a black or brown student is more likely to go to a segregated school than was the case in the 1960s.[4]

Of course, it is no news to students of color that they attend segregated schools; that information need not be mandated in the curriculum. We have selected the

---

4   Gary Orfield and Chungmei Lee, "Historic Reversals, Accelerating Resegregation, and the Need for New Integration Strategies," Report of the Civil Rights Project/ Proyecto Derechos Civiles, UCLA (August 2007), http:// civilrightsproject.ucla.edu/research/k-12-education/ integration-and-diversity/historic-reversals-accelerating -resegregation-and-the-need-for-new-integration -strategies-1/orfield-historic-reversals-accelerating.pdf.

teaching of *Brown vs. Board* in a segregated school as a representative anecdote specifically to point out the *cognitive* obstacles to understanding this lesson: "*Brown vs. Board* ended school segregation." What does that lesson mean? What does it imply? How are we to think about or even understand it? What are we to think of the people who teach us this lesson?

Robbing someone is unlawful. The police will arrest you. Driving without a license is illegal, or drinking before you are twenty-one, or smoking marijuana. If you do those things, you will be in trouble. *Brown vs. Board* made segregated schools illegal in the United States. Students are often shown film or photographs depicting federal troops or marshals enforcing the law against the illegal opposition of white people to school attendance by black students in Little Rock or Montgomery. But meanwhile the students watching these films are compelled to attend schools that are in fact segregated today, and all their lives have been compelled to attend segregated schools, and neither their parents, nor their teachers, nor their principals, nor the superintendent, school board, mayor, governor, or anyone else has ever, as far as they know, been in any trouble for what they are taught is a monumental, "landmark" illegality.

We are not pointing out that all students of color studying *Brown vs. Board* have these confusing thoughts, though many surely do. We are pointing out only that the state's purposes in mandating the teaching of *Brown vs. Board,* and the school's and teacher's purposes in implementing this "mandate," cannot conceivably coincide with the purposes of students who are sitting in the segregated classroom where *Brown vs. Board* is taught.

The authorities' official, but obviously disingenuous purpose is for the students to understand the healing of the Constitution and of the country through the process of constitutional amendment, judicial interpretation, and congressional legislation. But if the students in the segregated school have any interest at all in studying *Brown*, it would be to understand more thoroughly the hypocrisy, deceit, and abuse of power employed by the authorities and by the legal system in undermining attempts to make education more just.

No one—neither the students, nor the teachers, nor anyone else—can contemplate without puzzlement both the "mandated" lesson of *Brown vs. Board* and the fact of studying it in a segregated classroom. If the student or teacher is thinking at all, the contradiction between the lesson and the setting is bewildering, difficult or impossible to reconcile cognitively, like the visual confusions of the Escher drawing in which the stairs that take you up turn out to be the very same stairs that take you down. Looking at such a drawing, thoughtful people conclude there is a trick somewhere. Things are not what they seem. The surface hides a sinister depth. You look for awhile to try to find the trick, and then usually give up looking. Or you find it, or think you have found the trick, and bitterly begin to notice it being played on you over and over, even in places where before you had not imagined that you were fooled.

Or we could approach the problem from a slightly different point of view. How should the student interpret the rhetorical stance of the teacher's presentation of *Brown vs. Board*? The contradiction between the lesson and the reality of the segregated classroom establishes a context in which teachers cannot possibly mean what they say. The teacher's speech and the textbook's lesson must somehow figure a meaning beyond the literal meaning, because the literal meaning makes no sense in the segregated context.

If an actor on stage points to a stool and says, "This is my daughter," the audience immediately begins searching for a meaning that makes sense of the nonsense in context. The actor, too, must develop an interpretation of the line. In the theater where *Brown vs. Board* is taught, varying with the teacher's politics or purposes, the following stances or interpretations of the obviously counterfactual lesson all seem possible (more than one might apply for any given teacher on any given day):

1.   A patriotic stance: naïve, pompous, childishly, blindly swallowing the official line: "*Brown vs. Board* proves that segregated schools no longer exist in America. This country is great."

2.   An ironic stance: cynical, exposing the hypocrisy of the official line: "They tell us that *Brown* ended segregation, and I have to mouth this official doctrine, but we all understand this doctrine is a lie."

3.   A devoted stance toward the intentions of the *Brown* plaintiffs and toward the court's ruling, with a sober acknowledgment that though we have come a long way, we have a long way to go: "Thurgood Marshall was a great man, and the legal strategies leading to *Brown* were brilliant and far reaching. We must continue advancing this legacy by making the promise of *Brown* more real in the coming decades."

4.   A hortatory, moralizing stance: "People worked and died to achieve the breakthroughs of the Civil Rights era, such as *Brown,* and you students of color should appreciate the advances that have been made

by taking advantage of the opportunities offered to you to receive an education."

5.   A "scientific," objective stance: "The *Brown* ruling was read May 17, 1954, formally outlawing segregation in public schools. Remember that much for the test."

6.   A black separatist or black nationalist stance: "Despite the hypocrisy of *Brown's* inclusion in the curriculum, we're better off in this segregated space, because white people tend to mess things up, and we don't need them."

What is the student to think? How does the student judge or evaluate or question or even comprehend these stances? Each stance exposes the theatricality or burlesque of the curriculum; no interpretation of the lesson could be the literal communication of "fact" or "information" from teacher to student, since the "fact" that *Brown* ended school segregation is false. Even the purportedly "scientific," "objective" stance that the decision was announced and the plaintiffs won begs the question, why teach this "fact" rather than any of an infinite number of other "facts" that could be taught? The question must either be ignored or answered with reference to one of the other possible interpretations of the counterfactual claim that *Brown* ended segregation in schools.

A teacher's stance may be persuasive to an extent, depending on their authority and relation to the students. Or the teacher's attempt at interpreting the lesson for the students may be completely unpersuasive: the stool is just a stool, and the actor's calling it a daughter or son or anything else is incoherent, purposeless, nonsensical. Our point is that at best, the lesson of *Brown vs. Board* taught in the segregated class must be understood by the students as revealing deep duplicity in the curriculum and in the country's unifying myth—whether the duplicity is acknowledged by the teacher or not. At worst, the lesson is nonsense.

And what, at any rate, are the students to conclude about the celebratory tone of the integrationist fantasy? Do they conclude that they would be better off if they were in white people's schools? That there is something inferior about being separated off, as *Brown* itself says. Something wrong with the all-black or all-brown classroom because of an unspoken quality of being black or brown? Only the black separatist teachers or African nationalists take this bull by the horns and propound an opposite absolute: "You are better off *away* from white people, because they only confuse and corrupt things." In the all-white school or the "diverse" school of the suburbs, *Brown vs. Board* as a lesson in the curriculum is reassuring and comforting, because a country that has ended segregation in schools has obviously advanced the equal opportunity that underlies its ideals. But in the all-black school of the poor city, or the all-brown school, or the all black and brown school, *Brown vs. Board* as a lesson in the curriculum creates doubts, uncertainties, and hesitations, raising questions of what students are lacking, of what the schools are deficient in, and gives assurance only that the curriculum is not to be trusted.

How odd that students choosing not to invest themselves in the official lesson about *Brown* might be accused of rejecting learning for fear of acting white. If any student, white or otherwise, "learns" this topic in the state's curriculum, it can only be through papering over the truth that segregation in schools continues in strange new ways. Learning something untrue or misleading is an odd kind of learning. And if students of color reject the significance of *Brown*, seeing that it is actually insignificant in their lives, this is not because they reject learning, but because they reject what makes no sense and are offended by hypocrisy.

Faced with these predicaments, it seems rational for students to stay home, or skip class, or deny the teacher's authority over them, or refuse to read the assigned chapter or complete the assigned homework or answer the question when called on: "What is the significance of *Brown vs. Board* in the sequence of constitutional decisions on race?" We hope to have shown that a dignified silence in response to this question is not entirely inappropriate. But a dignified silence is very weak theater. We want a student to stand up on our stage and exclaim: "*Brown* precipitated the White Citizens Councils, white flight, the Republican Party's southern strategy, the geographic isolation of inner cities vis-a-vis white suburbs, and ultimately intensified segregation of public schools." This kind of exclamation might lead to more effective theater, but it is an answer not likely to win high marks on the standardized tests.

Our anecdote is intended only as representative of the predicaments facing young people in poverty when they find themselves compelled to attend schools that neither meet their needs nor serve their interests. There are many things even bad schools have to offer, and there are at least some good teachers in almost every school. Books are not that hard to come by, if a student cares to seek them out, and reading in itself can afford a wonderful education. But the official program of schools for young people in poverty is tainted and corrupt. The older the students get, the more convinced they become that the opportunities promised by school authorities are likely to be insubstantial, except for a very small part of the population. The problem of interpreting the teachers' stance toward the curriculum is rarely solved adequately in any class. A falseness underlies all the official topics, because they are said to "cover" what the students "need," but it would be much closer to the truth to say that the official topics hide what the students already know, namely that school asks them to "learn" many things that may be untrue and that seem useless.

Every child and every adolescent learns and desires to learn because they are human. This fundamental human purpose cannot change. But the purposes of schools for young people in poverty are not exclusively concerned with learning. They center instead on acceptance of a certain kind of authority and on the assignment of particular stations to particular people. Students are sorted into higher and lower reading groups. They are sorted into "advanced placement," "honors," "regular," and "special" math classes. They are sorted into college preparation, vocational, general, and alternative high schools. They are sorted into people promoted and people held back, into students on track to graduation and students "recovering credit," into students who have passed required tests and students who have failed them. But the older they get the more they realize that they are also sorted into students who go to private schools and students who do not; into students whose parents can drive them to school, and students who must take the bus; students who get free lunch, and students who can afford to buy lunch; students whose phones stay on, and those whose phones are often turned off; students who have clean clothes and new tennis shoes, and students whose clothes are dirty or old. The claim that some of these sortings make sense and others are arbitrary is lost on the large majority of young people in poverty. All appear arbitrary, or are accepted as representing an actual inferiority—the inferiority of poverty, or of stupidity, or of laziness, or of apathy, or of color. The lesson of *Brown vs. Board* can be taken as representative because it makes about as much sense as the whole range of sortings that students experience; the lesson of *Brown* says that color makes no difference in American education, but obviously it does; the lesson of schooling in general says that everyone who tries will succeed, but obviously they won't. Schools are segregated; learning is inequitably distributed and, in fact, scarce.

The problem students confront is therefore not how to learn as much as possible in school, but rather how to find something to do that makes sense—something that serves their own purposes, not the school's or the state's. Students addressing this problem have thrown the entire system of public education into turmoil. No matter how many times or how well *Dred Scott*, *Plessy*, and *Brown* are taught in class, students will fail to learn that the United States has ended educational segregation both because it has not ended segregation, and because students choose to advance their own interests and purposes, not the propagandistic and caste interests of the authorities.

What students in poverty would be more likely to find useful is an analysis of the contemporary version of Chief Justice Taney's pronouncement, that "the black man has no rights the white man is bound to respect." Today's schools say, in effect, "Poor students have no purposes their schools are bound to respect." In any contest between what students believe is in their interest and what adults and schools say is in their interest, the school must always win. If necessary, the students will be bribed, punished, expelled, or jailed, but in no case can they be permitted to succeed in advancing their own interests or purposes if those purposes conflict with the school's.

For wealthier clientele in private or better-off suburban public schools or in charters serving better-off students, the purposes of the school authorities dare not veer too drastically from the students' purposes because the disengagement of those students will quickly be followed by the disinvestment of their parents, which the schools literally cannot afford. But the purposes of students in poverty—for intellectual stimulation, for creative and artistic expression, for physical activity and adventure, for reliable nutrition, transportation and employment to participate fully in the life around them, and for opportunities to socialize, that is, to master the communicative norms and cooperative ways of the society they actually live in—these purposes are cruelly subordinated in their schools to the institutional purposes of maximizing control and predictability with regard to both their bodies and their minds.

That the students have no purposes the schools are bound to respect is a dictum thoroughly taught and learned at every level of education for young people in poverty. Thirst, hunger, excretion—the most private and basic needs of the biological organism—are regulated even for sixteen, seventeen, and eighteen-year-olds by the school authorities. It is very different in schools for wealthy young adults who do not need to argue with authorities about wanting to urinate and for whom ample time and opportunity are provided to nourish the body so that the mind can learn. Poor adolescents are not trusted to use the lavatory or to nourish themselves at will. They are treated as if they either do not know or will not tell the truth about their real purposes.

When these obvious and basic purposes of the physical organism are thwarted every day for millions of students in poverty, the more complex intellectual, emotional, and expressive purposes stand no chance at all. Speech and movement are forbidden unless explicitly permitted, the very opposite of the standard for a free citizenry. And it is difficult for someone who has only experienced the schooling of poor children in America to even conceive that schools might operate without regulations that treat the silent, immobile student as the ideal. But this silence and immobility is only a symptom of the underlying principle. Silence and immobility represent the absence of expressive purpose or motivation that the authorities assert as the condition of being a student: people who have no purpose that the school is bound to respect should be still until their teachers have taught them what purposes they are expected to have for that day, hour, and minute. This is Chief Justice Taney's legacy to the schools. The *Dred Scott* decision, in this sense, holds sway without reversal.

The heroic narrative of the Constitution's self-healing through amendment and judicial interpretation has unfortunately been encumbered by the drama of white flight, re-segregation by race and class, and the refinement and enlargement of systems to control the bodies and minds not only of students in schools, but also of millions caged behind bars, and threatened with imminent caging. The descendants of slaves do not meekly submit, and no narrative or re-framing will resolve the crises they provoke by their resistance. If these crises are to be resolved, it will be through fully moral acts of a dramatistic character,

through young people learning to demand that their interests be respected in massive, well-organized interruptions
of business-as-usual, through insurgency and the responses of the larger society to the insurgents.

PART III

The Idealized Algebra Project Classroom and the Practice of Dramatism

The representative anecdote of *Brown vs. Board* taught in a segregated school reflects the quandaries that result from treating young people in poverty as things rather than as persons. Empiricist or technocratic approaches can shed light on how a student's brain might "master the information" of *Brown vs. Board*, but those approaches cannot help us understand why people act the way they do. These "scientific" approaches cannot tell us why this student submits but that one rebels, nor which rhetorical stance the teachers will adopt, nor how the teachers and students will find themselves reacting to each other's autonomous actions. The acts of human beings require quite different modes of analysis than attending only to "what happens three minutes to three seconds before and three seconds to three minutes after the behavior." On the contrary, understanding how students or teachers act in these infernal schools requires an appreciation of the drama that is under way, and that has been under way, for years, or centuries, before the present action, and that will continue for years or centuries into the future. That appreciation must extend to all the elements of the drama: to the scene and material conditions; to the nature of the agents, their personalities and characteristics; to the styles, languages, and cultural forms available at just this time; to the various purposes that the drama might have or be conceived of as having; and to the creation—apparently without cause—of new acts, entirely unpredictable and surprising, like the act of a black person in America trying to walk into an all white school in the first place.[1]

The representative anecdote for a healed way of helping children grow up is not necessarily an experiment in a laboratory or the protocol for the delivery of a parcel, but the rehearsal of a play, the generation of a small drama or a series of small dramas within a larger collective action. We propose as an image the acts of younger people and older people pursuing a variety of purposes such that their acts coalesce, as in a play, into a shared assertion. We contend that divergent roles can collaborate toward an end that is both a part of the play's action and also beyond it.

It is as strange and inaccurate to say that the purpose of a classroom is to convey or transmit knowledge or skills as it is to say that the purpose of a play is for the audience to know what happens in the story. The story is of course necessary, but the play must also accomplish something real for the actors and audience. It should help to stabilize or hearten or purify or purge or re-form them in some way, as certainly Burke would argue. Both historically and substantially, plays are rituals in which actors and audience participate for collective purposes. A classroom, too, is a kind of ritual. If it is successful, it accomplishes an effect, both social and individual, that includes whatever knowledge or skill the students may

---

1 This list summarizes Kenneth Burke's "dramatistic pentad": Act, Agent, Scene, Agency, Purpose. See his *Grammar of Motives*.

learn, but that also reaches out to purposes and effects beyond the curriculum. This cold, hard fact about classrooms is obvious. Students and teachers are changed by what they do in schools. They not only know different things because of what they have learned, they also act differently because they have adopted and tested new personas in a dramatic context rich with other actors and influences. Often these new personas are corruptions of the child's native genius, but it is indisputable that school changes children far beyond the little they actually learn.

We have touched on the obstacles to a wholesome staging of the *Brown vs. Board* lesson in a segregated school. Now we want to describe a more successful, if somewhat idealized production which we will name an Algebra Project classroom, for reasons to be discussed below. The setting is still a segregated school for adolescents in poverty. And the subject matter, the "curriculum," could be algebra, geometry, trigonometry, or any other mathematics content that is normally "mandated" or at least "covered" in high school. The material assigned in the course and the particular characteristics of the students could be of many different kinds. Imagine whatever class you like. What is crucial is that the space of the classroom must be consecrated to the full development of the participants, to their active growth into roles that a wide and diverse audience well beyond the school walls will acknowledge as distinguished, noteworthy, and authoritative, at least to some degree.[2] The sense of despair and resignation, or despair and rage, that sits like lead or burning lead in our hearts must change by the ritual's end into a new emotion and purpose, after the

---

2   John Dewey, *The Later Works*, Vol. 7 (Carbondale: Southern Illinois University Press, 1984), 347.

symbolic drying up and sloughing off of hopelessness. The effects of this complex symbolic action will not be accomplished in a lesson or unit or semester, but may take many years—though discrete stages, like scenes from a play, will be distinguishable and effective in themselves. Our classroom of students stays together studying math as a cohort throughout high school, because their active growth cannot be chopped and parceled, but requires the continuities and cycles that all growing things require.

Although this classroom has actually existed for several years, we call it an "idealized Algebra Project classroom" not because its practices are completely worked out, but because the incipient nature of the work is, in itself, an ideal. The ideal and the real are not opposed. Many happy couples could be said to have ideal marriages, and those marriages are nevertheless entirely real. There may be imperfections in them, but coping with imperfection is one of the arts that happy couples study assiduously. So in the idealized classroom the question is not whether everything is perfect, but rather whether there is a method for harmonizing the problems that arise. The classroom is also called "idealized" because today's typical schools cannot tolerate it. Its ways offend the authorities. Nevertheless, it exists.

The student-actors are unlearned but eloquent, poor but sensitive to the nuances of social form, courtly in the respect that they attend in detail to the insignia of status. The king's and queen's court or the village council make use of forms of address or of precedence in seating, for example, that indicate distinct positions within the court's or council's hierarchy. Similarly the student-actors in our idealized Algebra Project classroom are alert to nuance of the same order. In this drama, the way a person walks, the lyrics they recite, the direction of their gaze when someone invites their attention, and various subtleties of tone and diction say a great deal about their roles in relation to each other and to the more authoritative characters in the play.

Note that "more authoritative characters" is plural and not the abstract singular "authority," because this ritual turns away from priestly or monarchical traditions whereby one actor mediates between the people and the mysteries of the celestial orders. In the priestly tradition of most contemporary schools, the teacher possesses knowledge, power, and authority conferred by an elaborately bureaucratized institution ordered in many ways like the Roman Catholic Church. In place of the pope, cardinals, bishops, and priests we have Secretaries of Education, school boards, superintendents, executive directors of this or that office, principals, vice principals, deans, and department heads, each legitimating and sanctioning, at least officially from the institutional point of view, the teacher's authority in the classroom as a singular representative of the entire order above it.

In our Algebra Project classroom, that priestly hierarchy is more or less ignored. The students are acknowledged as "the power in the room,"[3] and we conceive the drama in egalitarian, anticlerical terms, where anyone can suddenly find themselves in a position of authority for the moment.[4] The acquisition of authority in our classroom tends to follow a practice of collective discipline rather than of certification or official sanctioning. There are opportunities to demonstrate or exercise

---

3   Omo Moses, in conversation, 2008.
4   See the description of song leaders in Bernice Johnson Reagon, pages 24–25, above.

authority throughout the day, and each exercise of authority produces its own evidence of effectiveness or ineffectiveness that the individual and group can "read" if they choose. Successive attempts develop in an ordered way, constrained by the human and social result rather than by a certificate bestowed from above. When Darius proposes a method for finding the area of an n-gon, his demonstration is authoritative in the eyes of his peers for complex reasons emerging out of the ritual drama of the room.

DARIUS: Any regular polygon of n sides can be divided into n isosceles triangles, one triangle for each side. The area of each triangle can be found by multiplying the sine of 180°/n and the cosine of 180°/n.

TANISHA: Don't you need to multiply the height times the base by one-half to get the area of a triangle?

DARIUS: Yes, but each of the n triangles is made up of two smaller triangles congruent to each other, so you double the area of the smaller triangles, and 2 times ½ is just 1, leaving only the base times the height of the smaller triangle, which is the sine times the cosine of the ultra angle.[5]

---

5   The "ultra angle," is usually referred to as "half the central angle," by mathematicians, but the Algebra Project teaches students that the names of mathematical objects are made up by mathematicians, so students can make up names for mathematical objects, too, if they like. They must simply understand to use the more accepted names when they

Out of context, this exchange could be just a passage from a textbook in dialogue form. But Darius's authority in the classroom is not at all textual. It has been earned through dramatic exchanges over time. Similarly, there are authoritative co-teachers in the room: Twan, Sunshine, Wayne, X, B, and Maryland. They are graduates of the school who are now fighting their way through college, and even one "dropout" who chooses to explore the creation of this new dramatic context. The role of these co-teachers is to mentor, model individual and collective effort, and demonstrate by the money they earn teaching math that school might conceivably meet some actual material needs of young people in poverty.

The ritual drama is centered to some extent in the classroom, but stretches well beyond. The following scenes are far from exhaustive:

- Darius in bed, while the teacher knocks on the house door and calls to the open window from three floors below.
- Darius and Trey in Detroit at a radical social forum with their mentor, the co-teacher, B.
- Trey in the hall getting ready to fight over something someone texted him on his phone.
- Students at meetings during class, after school, or in the summer, learning to facilitate formal discussions, though they have never participated before in any meetings that were not disciplinary actions directed against them.
- Students meeting with public officials to demand better school food or to challenge the curriculum.

---

are in a different kind of public space. Dante made up the name "ultra angle," and many students, including Darius, now follow his usage in class.

- Chantel and Tanisha in Rhode Island at a youth conference.
- Swimming at the amusement park on the class trip.
- Marching to stop the construction of a new youth jail.
- Teaching math to elementary school students in the summer.
- Laughing and joking with peer mentors and teachers in the off-campus Algebra Project office.
- Cooking together in the school cafeteria.
- Collecting a paycheck for leading math study groups after school.
- Buying a set of weights for getting in shape.
- Learning to drive.

In the typical American classroom a small piece of instruction given by the teacher is said to "motivate" the students' participation in the lesson. In the Algebra Project classroom, we use a much more complex, dramatistic view of motive. We take the motive of students and teachers to comprise the entire circumstances of their lives as they understand and interpret them. The classroom is cut off only physically from the scenes enumerated above. But students and teachers understand, talk, and act with a complicated awareness that inside the classroom and beyond the classroom are interwoven and joined by intricate patterns and threads. The attenuated script of the typical lesson plan "brings in" the world outside in relatively simplistic ways, if it brings in the world at all. But even this simplicity is unnecessary because the world is already entirely within the room; the scientists' sterile classroom is infected from the very beginning by the human organism, by both the teachers and the students, who ineluctably carry around their biology, their culture, their purposes and intentions. The scene of the typical classroom is just the desks and chairs, the whiteboard and computers. The scene of the Algebra Project classroom shifts both from place to place and in scale, from a lonely soliloquy in an alley to the stage of the nation or even to the vast sky and ocean connecting America and Africa.

The anecdote of *Brown vs. Board* is one extreme of the attempt to cut the classroom off from the world. *Brown vs. Board* in a segregated school attempts to be a disembodied lesson. The students must literally restrict their gaze to their textbooks or they will notice the physical intrusion of the world into the "mandated" curriculum. They can't help seeing that the skin of their classmates contradicts the lesson. And the fact that the classroom and its mandates are necessarily a part of the world, not separated from it, forces both the teachers and the students to choose a rhetorical stance in relation to the curriculum. They must size up not just the lesson, but the lesson and the whole world. And then they must act. They, teachers and students, may act to subvert the lesson, to support it hypocritically, to support it provisionally, to welcome it ironically as evidence of the country's decay, to sleep through it, and so on. Our point is that their motivation involves an attitude and interpretation of the whole world, not merely an attitude and interpretation of the scripted lesson.

KAYLA: My father is getting out next May. He will be out in time to see me graduate.
MR. JAY: That's not as long as we feared.

We are not attempting to write a novel, nor to create fully rounded characters. For our purposes, the novel or novelistic journalism are somewhat misleading genres. They are dangerously specific, particular and concrete, but we are looking for anecdotes more generalizable and representative, better suited to the function of ritual. In the greatest novels, the particular and the universal may seem to coalesce, but great novels are relatively rare. Ralph Ellison wrote once: "I despise concreteness in writing."[6] Ellison was especially concerned with the function of imaginative writing as collective ritual, and so contrived a novel weighted toward abstraction and allegory: he devised an unnamed hero, Invisible Man, on the model of Everyman or Pilgrim or Brer Rabbit. And many of the novel's characters are overtly allegorical, like Supercargo, the enforcer of order on the otherwise unrestrained ids of the asylum patients, or Tod Clifton, whose first name represents, in German, a dead end. Ellison planned *Invisible Man* as a dramatistic enactment derived in Kenneth Burke's terms because he intended the novel to do something real for the nation. And as students of Ellison and Burke, we are also looking for an anecdote or representative classroom that will aid in the development of symbolic acts, of dramatic conversions, as opposed to the development of mere routines or protocols.

We could paint the picture of Kayla's family and might learn a great deal in the process. And we could generalize from the detailed picture to social and historical truths, if we chose. But the danger of such an approach is that our audience might believe that they now "know" or "empathize with" Kayla and her family and might interpret our purpose as novelistic entertainment

---

6   Ralph Ellison, *Shadow and Act* (New York: Vintage Books, 1972 /1953), 180.

or as a kind of journalistic reportage. This would be misleading. The function of a classroom, school, article, or essay is too often seen in our peculiar time as only to delight or to instruct. But a dramatistic approach to education intends to build on those terms by adding a third stage: to move to action, or more formally, to induce action in beings that by nature respond to symbols.

We are interested in working out how Kayla or Darius or Tanisha will decide, individually and collectively, to put more time and effort into doing mathematics as part of a strategy to help them fashion an insurrection in their schools, to interrupt the educational arrangements that do not meet their needs, and to devise new arrangements for both education and the larger society. Although the details of working this out are and will be personal for each of them, we are at the same time attempting to develop a terminology and communicative norms that will allow the students, their teachers, and parents to share a common purpose and to act in ways that advance the common good.

G.P. [*loudly*]: Get the fuck out of my face!

MR. JAY [*sitting beside G.P., calmly, but intensely*]: If you rotate this figure 90°, do you think angle B will lie exactly on top of angle D?

G.P. [*a little quieter*]: Get the fuck out of my face.

MR. JAY [*putting his hand gently on G.P.'s shoulder*]: Maybe try it with the tracing paper and see what happens. And remember not to cuss.

G.P.: I said don't touch me. [*Moving his face very close, emphatically, but now quietly*] No.

During this exchange, the other students and peer co-teachers, scattered around the room, are involved in several of their own conversations about the geometric figure; no one displays any alarm at G.P.'s vehemence.

This bit of dialogue fits well in our idealized classroom. The ideal we are advancing is not disconnected from reality. It is an ideal of human relations, not of cause and effect. In the ideal of cause and effect, the skilled teacher asks what technique or technology can "extinguish" G.P.'s undesirable behavior. The idealized Algebra Project teacher, in contrast, is not even sure whose problem G.P.'s behavior is. It is a problem, because it is getting in the way of his learning about rotational symmetry. But conceived as a play or drama, rather than as a failed "intervention," the moment is quite interesting.

Played a certain way the obscenity could provoke anxiety in some audiences by violating taboos relating to teachers or adults as authorities in relation to young people. And because G.P. is classed as black in America and Mr. Jay is classed as white, the exchange also implies a charged question about whether the characters or audiences will racialize their interpretation of the motives and plot dynamics involved.

Or the scene could provoke judgments about the teacher's apparent "permissiveness." The liberal white teacher could be seen as demonstrating both a lack of knowledge about black cultural norms (G.P.'s behavior is culturally unacceptable in a classroom), and also an essentially racist acceptance of the black student's lack of learning. The white teacher "allows" the black student to fail. Or the same interpretation might be applied in non-racialized terms: the teacher-authority "allows" the student-dependent to fail.

Or the scene could be played as a straight rebellion, with G.P. in the role of Caliban, heroically attempting to undermine the power-hungry, patronizing, and dominion-seeking Prospero-like teacher.

We are proposing, however, a different reading of the scene, one that fits better with the wider context. For first of all, the other students and co-teachers don't react in ways that would be consistent with any of the alternatives above. They register no awkwardness or discomfort at the violation of the taboos, nor do they jump in to support their black brother in a confrontation with white authority. They don't even laugh at the outright disrespect. (In fact, we could have assigned the line, "Remember not to cuss," to one of the students, except that at this point in the exposition, we want to avoid the appearance that the students are very well behaved; they may all curse like sailors, though usually for purposes of emphasis and humor, rather than for expressing anger.) And the students testify to the general academic seriousness of the room, as opposed to an atmosphere of apathy, by remaining engaged in their own conversations about geometry, more or less ignoring G.P.'s potentially distracting role.

There is also the wider context of G.P. and Mr. Jay's relationship outside of the classroom that emerges from other scenes: G.P. confiding to Mr. Jay that his girlfriend is pregnant. Mr. Jay waiting with G.P. in the crowded hallway outside the detention center courtroom, or discussing with G.P.'s public defender the story of his successes in the Algebra Project; Mr. Jay visiting G.P. and his girlfriend in the hospital to see their newborn son; Mr. Jay and G.P. in the gas station lot, when G.P. tells him that his grandmother has cancer; Mr. Jay watching G.P. play basketball at summer camp and then checking off his name on the form for free lunches.

With these scenes as background, the student's aggression toward the teacher and the teacher's "permissiveness" may be interpreted differently. Kenneth Burke describes the standoffishness or social awkwardness that inevitably accompanies communication between distinct groups of people.[7] In this case, there are a number of complexly related group differences: old vs. young; teacher vs. student; middle class vs. working class; white vs. black; expert vs. novice; and possibly others. G.P.'s vehemence may be partly a result of his naïve openness about the social embarrassments caused by the multiple class distinctions. That is, if we interpret G.P.'s motive not as intending rudeness or disrespect, and not as defiance, we might be able to see his speech as revealing a kind of extreme sensitivity to the complications of the social differences. He is not yet skilled enough to put these sensitive feelings into adequate language, but he would nevertheless like to if he could. Certainly, he makes himself present, rather than running away. Other young people in similar predicaments might take refuge in silence. Chantel, for example. But most good teachers know instinctively or have learned that outbursts or silences from students with whom they otherwise have warm relations are often signs of the general difficulty in all human relations, and especially the difficulty, in certain circumstances, of communicating well with someone you love or respect, but who is socially of a different status, gender, or kind.

---

7   Burke, *A Rhetoric of Motives*, 208–209.

The corrupted atmosphere of American schools for young people in poverty makes complex, intimate communication between teachers and students nearly impossible. That it happens at all is evidence of almost miraculous ingenuity and good will, and it happens thousands of times every day all across the country. But this successful communication occurs in places and ways, by signs and tokens, that are generally illicit, or at least problematic. The official, institutional doctrine maintains that communication between teachers and students should be straightforward and literally independent of the identity of either student or teacher. Of course, enlightened educators understand that they must "know their students." But this ingredient of evidence-based teaching practice is simply data the teacher uses to choose the appropriate intervention for producing the selected behavior required by the curricular mandates. There is no room in the official, institutional doctrine for either the student's or the teacher's awkwardness, embarrassment, confusion, or what we could call generally "blushing" caused by their human awareness that they occupy different positions in quite complex hierarchies, but are thrown together to do difficult and intimate work.

In the Algebra Project classroom, on the other hand, this awareness is always acknowledged as a central element of dramatic design. We are studying geometry as a stage in our mutual development, but the ultimate goal is to find adequate terms for the consubstantiality that we feel grounds us as participants in a common insurgency.

We are not denying the awkwardness of "Get the fuck out of my face." We are saying only that awkwardness might be appropriate when so many obstacles to effective communication are present. The obstacles are deeply ingrained in the caste structure of the country, and being committed to overcoming those obstacles, we anticipate and expect that what looks like the breaking of taboos or disrespect or cultural misunderstanding will be ordinary features of a classroom drama that explores the destruction of caste. We understand these expressions and outbursts not as employing static or literal terms, but rather as carrying meanings that can only be interpreted dialectically in relation to other terms, expressions, incidents, and actions. Every good teacher knows that a student's obscenities can mean "I need your help," and that "No!" in certain contexts can mean an emphatic, "Yes!"

The end of education is not knowledge for its own sake, but doing together what needs to be done. Paolo Freire has inspired many of us with his way of expressing this idea: that we are not concerned with teachers pouring colonial narratives into the empty heads of the students; we are concerned with transforming the world. In even the most outrageous of our schools, people "do something" together; we never stop being human. It is just that what we do in these schools is forced and coerced and perpetuates the world, rather than transforming it through passionate collaboration.

An intimate familiarity with schools makes us aware of other ways that G.P.'s outbursts might be dealt with:

G.P.: Get the fuck out of my face.
MR. STEVENSON [as the other students look up, laugh, shriek; general excitement]: I'm writing you up. Go to the office.
G.P.: Suck my dick.

[Mr. Sevenson picks up the phone.[8] G.P. knocks over a desk and exits to the hall, hurrying away to avoid the police.]

Is it relevant to G.P.'s motivation in this scene, or not, that his father has spent many years in prison, that his brother, a year older, is in jail awaiting trial for murder, that G.P. himself has been locked up half a dozen times for selling drugs?

Given Mr. Stevenson's reaction—a common enough response to such outbursts—there is little room for G.P. to experiment with new terminology for the circumstances that confront him. Violence and coercion sit so nearby that he can feel their breath on his neck day and night. He is required by the judicial authorities to carry a box with him as a device for the tracing of his position on earth, and as a constant reminder that his hands may be bound in a moment, that a cage awaits him. I have heard a very loving and kind woman, a vice-principal who became frightened of Tristian—when he was enraged at being forbidden from using the lavatory—taunt him with her power to have him cuffed and confined.

In this everyday drama, everyone already knows their roles. It is an almost unbearably tedious rehearsal day after day, except for the amusing interludes of emotional

---

8   The teacher's picking up the phone in the schools we are discussing has become a Pavlovian signal. It is so frequently followed shortly after by the entrance of police or "security" officers into the classroom that the mere act of the teacher picking up the phone generates an emotional and probably a hormonal reaction in many students, an increase, for example, in the level of the stress hormone, cortisol. (The increase in cortisol levels was suggested in conversation by Prof. Jessica Ruglis, now at McGill University.)

blood-letting that can occasionally flare into physical violence if one party or another "takes things too far."

We are rehearsing a different drama, though in the context of and set against that ordinary one, exploring unexpected lines and gestures, or lines and gestures delivered in unexpected ways. This allows G.P. or Tristian to adjust and refine their terminology, their motivation, as they deliberate on how to proceed. In Mr. Stevenson's classroom their range of action is "comply" or "defy." But in the idealized Algebra Project classroom the students' range of possible actions is almost infinitely greater and includes virtually anything people might do together who share a common purpose.

There is a brittleness in the false schools and classrooms. Both the teachers and the students expect things to break apart or shatter. Outbursts often result in violence or threats of violence. Questions are often rejected or ignored, whether because the teacher doesn't notice the question, or has no time for it, or has no answer. So students stop asking questions and the dramatic exchanges die into silence.

Tests result often in "failure," but "pass or fail" is a brittle pair. A three-year-old who says, "I sawed a dog," doesn't "fail" in any way; she knows many things, but also has things she doesn't yet know, like the irregular past tense of "see." We smile; we don't say, "wrong"; we gently correct by repeating, "You saw a dog?" A high school student, however, who knows many things, but not "enough" as measured by some completely arbitrary quantification, is said to "fail," a discouraging result to anyone who has experienced it. And failing tests results "naturally" in the segregation of "good" students from "bad" students, first into different reading groups, then into different classes,

space and continuity in time, versions of the standard
Aristotelian unities that distinguish a competent drama.
It is the fear of being affected by the other that fractures
these unities and poisons our schools. Caste segregation is the visible form of that fear. Different "kinds" are
rarely brought together for long. And the technocrat's
doctrine that no student is or could be competent to interrupt, derail, or throw off-balance an expert's lesson is
a psychological defense against the embarrassments of
caste. Confronting the embarrassments of caste openly
and honestly begins with an acknowledgement of uneasiness, the recognition that there is another *person* in
the room affecting you, another presence on the stage.
But the technocracy prefers to clear the stage of active presences, as if the uneasiness were caused by the
offending student's behavior, which can be banished,
rather than by the offending student's reality and personhood, the human stain, permanent and indelible.

Note that "instruction" doesn't end simply because
G.P. behaves outrageously. The other students continue
to discuss rotational symmetry with their own teams.
And Mr. Jay continues to explore approaches G.P. might
take to move forward while pointing out that his language may violate the decorum of the scene. The nature
of the ritual is such that G.P.'s cussing, or any other action initiated by a student short of violence, can be incor-
porated into the dialogue by an adjustment of terms and
suppleness of the actors' responses. This means devising
a rhetoric of inclusion to engraft G.P.'s language to the
stock of the class and see him as advancing rather than
as opposing the classroom's collective goals. In the drama
of a healthy family, the small child's tantrums are not
catastrophic, but a "stage" that the child moves through

toward a more sophisticated relation to authority. In fact, the healthy family recognizes the tantrums as necessary to the development of an identity that is both independent and respectful of community. The child who doesn't resist at all is as much "at risk" as the child who never stops resisting. In short, there are many ways to treat an outburst as an opportunity in a developmental sequence, rather than as a crime.

In *A Grammar of Motives*, Kenneth Burke highlighted the developmental relation between "action," "suffering," and "understanding.": "The act organizes the opposition (brings to the fore whatever factors resist or modify the act)...the agent thus 'suffers' this opposition and as he learns to take the oppositional motives into account, widening his terminology accordingly, he has arrived at a higher order of understanding."[9] This three-stage process that Ellison used in *Invisible Man* (and explicitly attributed to Burke) describes both the teachers' and the learners' actuality in the Algebra Project classroom.[10] The acts of students in schools, no less than the acts of teachers and administrators, "organize the opposition." What is disastrous is that the brittle opposition of the bureaucratic school organizes itself again and again in ways that pretend not to be affected by the actions of the students. Correspondingly, the students organize themselves in ways that pretend not to be affected by the school. And so, in accordance with the medieval formula that Burke cites approvingly, *intelligere est pati* (to understand is to be affected by), neither party understands much differently at the end of the scene than they did at the beginning. One of the meanings Burke cites for *pati*

9   Burke, *A Grammar of Motives*, 39.
10   Ellison, *Shadow and Act*, 176–177.

is "to permit."[11] His dramatistic formula thus becomes, "to understand is to permit" or "to permit and so to be affected by." Mr. Jay "permits" G.P.'s cussing, and so allows himself to be affected by it (though not in the expected way), and so learns to understand and respond to G.P.'s "organized opposition" in ways that he could not have come upon if G.P. were simply "disciplined" and excluded. In return, G.P. permits Mr. Jay to question him about geometry, permits Mr. Jay to care about him, and to call him G.P., which stands for "Good Person" and alludes to his role as both hero and gentle father, a sign in language that student and teacher share a common purpose and move themselves toward it, though haltingly and with embarrassments that are not entirely in either's control.

The greatest obstacles to this ideal are the teacher's shame at not being able to "control" the class and the students' uneasy conviction that they are the kind of creatures that need to be controlled. This shame and conviction derive from deeply internalized values, or perversions of values, and chiefly from the perversion that any student's autonomous intentions, desires, or acts should be "extinguished" and then converted into an intention, desire, or act of the teacher's. The Algebra Project would banish this perversion in our dramatism and accept instead that in a living ritual the various characters represent sometimes competing principles that can nevertheless share the same stage and purposes, though cast as contraries at the level of the "story." To maintain the illusion of control, teachers, schools, and bureaucracies exclude the people that affect them autonomously and independently. The Algebra Project class, in contrast, is wild with affection, expressed in all the paradoxical and

11 Burke, *A Grammar of Motives*, 40.

counterlogical ways of our symbol-using species. We welcome the juxtaposition of contesting principles and believe for logical, dialectical reasons that the contest of principles is not dangerous in itself, nor is it a shame to be affected by another human being.[12]

Trey cradles Dakayla with his left hand while holding her bottle in his right. Sunshine, Dakayla's mother, is helping Tanisha make a chart to show how the sine function is related to properties of similar triangles.

```
TREY [to Sunshine]: Hand me the bib.
SUNSHINE [getting up to give the bib to
    Trey, but addressing Tanisha]: What do
    we know about the ratio of corresponding
    sides when two figures are similar?
TANISHA: Similar figures have common ratios
    for corresponding sides.
SUNSHINE: And what do we know about corre-
    sponding angles of similar figures?
TANISHA: They are the same, too.
TREY: Does it have to be some kind of right
    triangle to use the sine?
TANISHA [pointing]: The baby just spit up on
    your pants, Trey.
SUNSHINE [waiting for TREY to wipe his pants
    with the bib]: Why do you think that
    might be true?
PRINCIPAL FARMER enters the classroom car-
    rying a walkie talkie.
PRINCIPAL FARMER [looking at the scene
```

---

12 For more on "counterlogical," see William Kurtz Wimsatt, *The Verbal Icon* (Lexington, KY: University of Kentucky, 1954), 201.

*disapprovingly, not pausing long enough
to hear any of the math*]: Babies are not
allowed in the school building. If something happens, we have no insurance.

TANISHA: We always have babies in here. What
is someone supposed to do if their child
care falls through?

JASMINE: It's better to come to school and
do your math than to stay home and get behind, even if you have to bring your baby.

Another realization of the Aristotelian unities in the
Algebra Project classroom is that the ritual is geographi-
cally rooted and respects families, the continuity of generations across time. The Algebra Project evolved out of the
dusty towns of the Mississippi Delta, where black people
learned to see themselves as actors on the national stage
and forced the world to act back. Bob Moses explains
that the young, inexperienced organizers who shook the
foundation of the white power structure in the south
used some very basic methods that they learned from Ella
Baker: Go somewhere that feels dangerous, no matter
how distant it seems to be from centers of power, and stay
put.[13] Let the families that have abided there for generations show you what is important. They will try to protect
you, and you will try to protect spaces for them to act in
ways that make sense to them. The high and mighty will
find themselves reacting to the lowly and honorable. That
will create opportunities for learning and new action.

---

13 Charles Payne, *I've Got the Light of Freedom: The Organiz-
    ing Tradition and the Mississippi Freedom Struggle* (Berke-
    ley: University of California Press, 2007), 84–102; Moses
    and Cobb, *Radical Equations.*

Black Mississippians had the vote in the 1870s, but they lost it at the hands of the most violent and successful uprising against the rule of law in American history, executed by the White Liners and other saboteurs of Reconstruction.[14] The knowledge of this loss had been passed down in certain black Mississippi families, churches, and political organizations for almost a hundred years when the insurgent young people of SNCC, and the Congress of Racial Equality (CORE), moved in and stayed put. They thought they were going to work on desegregating lunch counters and public accommodations, but the old folks in the Delta said getting the vote back was much more important. So Bob Moses and his young organizers went to places like the plantation where Fannie Lou Hamer worked, and asked her and people like her if they wanted to go try to register to vote. Some did. For wanting to vote, they were thrown out of work and out of their homes, had their food cut off, were beaten, sent to jail, and sometimes killed. But their act, this total assertion of organizing to vote, drew out a reaction from frightened white people and exposed weaknesses in the system of racism. The young people, the sharecroppers, domestic workers, and day laborers exploited those weaknesses, exposed the country's hypocrisy, at least for a while, and some important things changed.

Geography is significant: Fannie Lou Hamer lived most of her life in Sunflower County, whose dominant land-owner happened to be James Eastland, Chairman of the Judiciary Committee of the United States Senate. Senator Eastland was an enormously influential lynchpin in racist control of federal and state power, but found

---

14 Nicholas Lemann, *Redemption: The Last Battle of the Civil War* (New York: Farrar, Straus and Giroux, 2007), p .

himself compelled to respond to Mrs. Hamer because the SNCC workers and Mrs. Hamer dug in and stayed put. The Babylonian tower that Senator Eastland sat atop of relied for its stability on a base of black people and poor people that it crushed with its weight. But when those poor black people agitated, the tower lost its stability. This is the destabilizing effect of a massive, popular insurgency. Senator Eastland could not prevent the challenge of Mrs. Hamer and the Freedom Democratic Party to the all-white Mississippi delegation to the Democratic Party Convention in 1964. And the Democratic Party was therefore forced open and changed its rules in significant ways, and white southern men are still resentfully strategizing to get their power back from black people today. Later in her life, Mrs. Hamer, youngest of twenty children in her family, dedicated herself to end the forced sterilization of women, a crime of which she was herself a victim.

We try to pass this generational wisdom along in the Algebra Project classroom. In the backwater halls of the infernal schools, the students, teachers, and organizers must dig in and stay put. Babies are a joy in our homes; if they show up in our classrooms, they are a joy there, too. They get there because their mother or father or sister or brother or cousin or whichever young person is caring for the child has put themselves physically in the place where they might change themselves through learning, and the baby goes where they go. The student wanting so badly to be at that spot on earth is a good thing. The student caring for a little one is also a good thing. Far from being a sign of disarray or lack of focus, the babies in the classroom are a sign of values that rank well up in the hierarchy of values we all share.

There are other values that might seem opposed to wanting to be present in the classroom and wanting to care for a child, but that are simply less important under the circumstances of our play. True, babies can be a distraction. And we might value trying to avoid distractions while learning geometry or algebra. But if this means certain actors in our ritual will not be able to participate, we have only avoided the distraction at the expense of a more significant discontinuity, the student's complete exclusion from the act. It would be nice if high-quality child care were more readily available, but Wayne and Mahogany, for example, have discovered a troublesome bureaucratic threshold: if they accept food stamps, they no longer qualify for free day care, but if they accept free day care, they no longer qualify for food stamps. Maybe we will change these regulations one day, but in the meantime, their babies are welcome in our classroom.

The difference between a dramatistic approach to education and a technocratic approach shows up very clearly in Principal Farmer's objection: the little ones are not covered by the school's insurance. In technocracy, alternative ethical choices are compared quantitatively and especially through monetization. Dakayla's visit to the classroom is potentially very expensive, because the risk involved in her presence is too great to be included in the actuarial tables. The cost of forbidding her visit, on the other hand, seems to be zero. At worst, if a student can't attend school because she must care for a child elsewhere, there is only the effect of the absence on Principal Farmer's attendance data to be reckoned, something very small compared with a lawsuit that could run into the millions. Principal Farmer may also have some concern for the baby's safety in the "persistently dangerous" high school, even though the Algebra Project classroom is a place of love and shared purpose that is almost certainly more sheltered than many of the streets Sunshine and Dakayla walk down to get home. Nevertheless, the objection that the principal voices is about the insurance because that objection is decisive. Any intention that runs afoul of the monetized insurance risk is, for that reason alone, not only a bad intention, but almost impossible, unimaginable, forbidden. In a dramatistic approach, however, the highest values involve preserving the unity of action: "Let them be together, even if we run afoul of the lawyers and actuaries."

For technocrats, the requirements of insurance policies are the highest priority. Next come "measurable results," and especially test scores. Great advances in monetization of learning have been made over the last two decades. What was previously only whispered about in technocratic covens has now become a reality: the test scores of Mr. Smith's students can be compared using complex algorithms with the test scores of Ms. Brown's students in ways that are said to take account of the expected variability in the students' backgrounds, prior experiences, and socioeconomic status. Mr. Smith's "value added" can be ranked relative to Ms. Brown's "value added," and one will be paid more than the other.[15]

Urban education in the twenty-fist century is emphatically an economic transaction whether the school is public or private. The monetizing of education seems to "liberate" the ritual of schools from geography through the portability of money: this principle is formulated as, "funding follows the child." Children are now a kind

---

15 For Value Added Metric in teacher evaluation, see Darling-Hammond et al, *Getting Teacher Evaluation Right.*

of currency, and principals are taught to "market" their schools to parents so that the parents will "invest" in the school by driving their child there—an average benefit to an American school today of approximately $9,000. Schools lose business or gain business just as grocers or gas stations do. Students in many schools now come from all over, not just from the community in which the school is located.

Rather than pursue a clash of principles and ethical dilemmas with the characters who find themselves at the neighborhood school, the theoretically "efficient" school system distributes monetized quanta of teachers and learners here and there. Just as with twenty-first century labor and capital markets, so with education: everything is in flux. Schools are closed; schools are opened; teachers and students reassigned as if they had no roots. But they do have roots. They are rooted in their human relationship with each other and they are rooted in their natural relation to the earth as a physical and cultural scene of action.

Families are the conservative social form resisting the fragmenting, disintegrative tendency of "markets." Though this topic is immense, we are highlighting the features of a dramatic production in contrast to the features of a scientific experiment, a market equilibrium, or a behavioral protocol. The familial as a category of thought and action intersects in many ways with the genre of drama. Families are conservative both in the sense that they are the oldest social form and in that their primary function is preservation either of genetic features (from a biological point of view) or of values, languages, and traditions (from an anthropological point of view). Historically, drama as an artistic genre develops out of religious rituals when individualistic motives begin to challenge the cohesion of families or tribes. In our time, such motives have hypertrophied and often overwhelm the familial. The function of artistic and literary representation as vehicles for resolving this kind of tension is an important topic. But our purpose here is to see public education as public ritual, dramatic in form, and ordered so that the individual's relation to the social and familial can be worked out in relative safety. Otherwise, we will be left with only money and test scores as the means of comparing conflicting values, clearly inadequate tools for the resolution of tension between the individual and the group, for example, or between men and women, youth and age, too fast and too slow, or rich and poor.

With these dramatistic thoughts in mind, we encourage students and teachers in the idealized Algebra Project classroom to think of their families as a part of the small society that we are creating as our play. Children aren't sacrificed. Caregivers aren't secluded from those who are childlessly able to get ahead. We do not want some to do well and some to do badly. We want, rather, to counter contemporary individualism with a more communal and familial emphasis, engaging the conflict between individualism and collectivism, or child-oriented and child-free, and working toward resolution of these conflicts through the full and creative presence of the competing factions.

For these reasons, the Algebra Project classroom in its extensive venues teaches the three tiers of demand.

Dante is walking home from school alone after rehearsing with his team. The team is preparing a workshop for young people learning to organize. They will earn $500 for the workshop.

DANTE: Tristian should have been there today. The workshop is just three days away. I'd call him, but my phone's off. I really need some of that $500. Why wasn't he in school? He's supposed to lead the part about how we rely on each other. [Laughing] That's ironic. I used to be like that. I'd miss school because it was raining, or because I stayed up all night playing a game. Now I go to school every day. "Dante," I say, "get out of bed. Dante, get your clothes on. Dante, get out of the house and start walking." Tristian still playing games, making excuses. I'll borrow my sister's phone and call him. Maybe Cam can call him, too. He listens to Cam. If we do well at this workshop, we might get invited to do some more and earn more money. Now where's my sister?

Demand on yourself. Demand on your peers. Demand on the larger society. This is an ordered series: the first is prerequisite to the second, the second is prerequisite to the third. Demands on peers to come to school are hollow if the people making the demand skip school themselves. And democracies require "earned insurgencies": attempts to change the unjust arrangements of a society will be crushed unless the insurgents have developed a discipline that can withstand the oppressor's attempts to fracture their unity and weaken their organization.[16] This discipline and resilience earns the respect of

16 Moses, keynote address, Creating Balance Conference, New York, 2007.

wide-ranging segments in society, and the contribution of push from below and unexpected allies in key places can disrupt or at least complicate the normal use of state violence, as in the abolition or civil rights movements.

Bob Moses describes how the struggle for voting rights required both the courage of individuals to go down to the courthouse in small Delta towns and attempt to register to vote—a demand on oneself—and also the courage to invite others to attempt to register, to learn about the obstacles to voting, and to develop and implement collective strategies for overcoming those obstacles. The demand on the federal government and on the country to enforce the fifteenth amendment's guarantee of the right to vote was only satisfied because a significant portion of the country's middle-class white population were persuaded to act by the ethical example of sharecroppers and domestic workers making these prior demands on themselves and on their peers, despite the brutality they faced. The point was won only when, in 1964, the Mississippi Freedom Democratic Party, riding on the tide of Freedom Summer, effectively prevented the national Democratic Party Convention in Atlantic City from conducting its business. Southern whites, clinging to power, claimed that colored people were content to allow whites to determine political questions on their behalf. But the acts of black people braving assault, imprisonment, unemployment, and the risk of death gave the lie to the racist claim that they were apathetic about politics.

So, today, we hear that young people in poverty are apathetic about their education, that they don't come to school, don't do homework, don't respect their teachers, deride those who study as "acting white," and that their parents don't care either. To reverse these stereotypical views what is required is not only the well-publicized examples of individual students who "against the odds" make demands on themselves to comply with the requirements of schools, but a deliberate building of both the first two tiers of demand: the "rhetoric of address to the self," as Burke calls it, to come on time, pay attention, put time and effort into learning, and also the demand on your peers to understand the significance of these personal and collective struggles. Only when these two tiers are mastered will the strategy become clear to the mass of society, as it did in the voting rights struggle, that the young people are demanding what everyone says they don't want. At that point, a mass movement to interrupt the educational system has a chance of succeeding, rather than being crushed outright by state violence. This at least is the pattern of the breakthrough in voting rights that has enabled, for example, a black nationalist to be elected mayor of Jackson, Mississippi—again, not necessarily a goal in itself, but certainly a powerful organizing tool.

It is not the demand on the larger society, but the demand on peers that is the beginning of political action. The language "demand on peers" is unfamiliar. But it is another way of saying "self-government" or "democracy." Of course, we are not describing contemporary political arrangements in the United States when we use the word "democracy." We are describing a practice aimed at as a goal in many radical groups, and pretended to— often cynically—in local, state, and federal governments. Monarchy or autocracy or oligarchy or dictatorship are forms of government where the ruler makes demands on the people; demands come from above. But, in principle, a democracy has a different structure of demand.

Contests between citizens of a principled democracy are between peers. If prosecutors charge citizens with a crime, they are charging their peers, and a jury of peers will decide guilt or innocence. If legislators enact laws or executives enforce laws, they are acting on behalf of and in relation to a class of citizen to which they themselves belong, at least in theory. If a group of citizens petition the government of a principled democracy, they are petitioning people who are not "above" them, but who "represent" them. If citizens fail to abide by the laws of a true democracy, they implicitly contest the authority not of the king, but of their fellow citizens.

Our social forms are very far from this ideal today. Not only is political "democracy" a farce and parody of participatory governance, but in other social settings, the idea of making demands on peers is strange and foreign. The typical pattern of demand is from "above" to "below." In employment, in both public and private bureaucracies, in most churches and in schools, bosses or authorities make demands on workers or subordinates, limited sometimes by "grievance procedures" or regulations that do not, however, change the relation of who is doing the demanding and who is responding to demands.

The great majority of citizens in our "democracy" have not begun to imagine that workplaces or schools could be democratic. Even the adults in schools accept the absolute authority of the principal and follow "mandates" that they themselves had no role or representation in formulating. Teachers, in most public schools at least, do not see themselves as peers of administrators or superintendents. They are subordinates and risk charges of insubordination if they do not obey. The idea that high-school students should see themselves as peers of their teachers or administrators is even more outlandish. Even at age eighteen, when they are electoral peers of the older adults as a matter of law, the students' relation to school authority is still entirely dependent and subordinate.

In contrast, the three tiers of demand in the Algebra Project amount to a reversal of the direction of authority; the practice of building small, self-determining units is radical preparation for larger scale action in the future, developing an insurgency. Networks of truly democratic organizations and small institutions can release the power necessary to massively interrupt dominant institutions, forcing them to collapse, at least temporarily, while new arrangements emerge. This is not only an idealistic theory. It is a realistic description of what has happened in the world many times. The insurgent runaway slaves, for example, freed themselves, an utterly demanding practice, sometimes simply as individuals, but more commonly in association with their peers. These acts required planning, coordination, precision, patience, fortitude, and the ability to make shared decisions in strained circumstances as smaller or larger collectives. Many of the freed slaves then organized to form all kinds of formal and informal institutions, not only to support and encourage more runaways, but to create churches, schools, publications, business, and political associations that undergirded the abolition movement. These insurgent acts eventually led to the conditions for the dramatic contest between freedom and the fugitive slave laws, and eventually to the convulsions of the Civil War.

We are discussing how this style of action might emerge or grow in representative classrooms that are dedicated to the education of citizens in a democracy. When Vincent Harding says "we are practitioners in an

educational system that does not yet exist," he is referring
to these tiers of demand. America, the democratic ideal,
an educational system that brings young people up into
the ritual of making demands on themselves, on their
peers, and on the larger society, does not yet exist; but
the enactment of these kinds of demands, the day-in,
day-out work of their practitioners, is growing already
in many places.

The class meets to discuss a problem.

SHONTRICE: Who is facilitating today?

CAM: I will, where's the agenda?

SHONTRICE: I wrote it on the board.

CAM [*reading*]: First, we're going to talk
about who will work four days a week
after school and who will only work two
days. We can't afford both. Who has an
idea about that?

JEFFREY: I think the people who worked here
the longest should get the most hours.

TANISHA: But that doesn't help us to develop
new leadership or get the younger people
to take on more responsibility.

DANTE: Now that I'm 17, my mother says I'm
supposed to bring more money into the
house. Most ninth graders don't have that
kind of pressure. I need more hours.

SHONTRICE: What's the total budget for this
site?

KAYLA: $15,000.

CAM: So, how many people can we hire for
four days?

DANTE: Sunshine did a spreadsheet and laid

This legal crawl space made room for the other kind of crawl space, too: places to rehearse while getting ready for the larger public performance. These were the churches, the porches and stoops, the homes of brave people where ordinary sharecroppers, domestic workers, and students could come together to learn how to struggle, how to make collective decisions, and how to articulate political demands. People who come to consensus on a chunk of work that needs to get done can also learn how to organize themselves to do it. But that takes time and physical meeting places with relative security for studying issues, making mistakes, testing ideas and roles, assessing progress, and regrouping after defeat. Our idealized classroom, the Algebra Project youth offices off-campus, forums, conferences, and gatherings, in our own city and elsewhere, are exactly such locations. You don't need to rush someone who is about to learn to walk. You just need to protect a space for them to crawl around in till they're ready to try standing up. For adolescents, nothing is more important than trying on personas and rehearsing roles. They do this whether they are permitted to do it or not. They will provoke and observe reactions to their experimental acts, reflect on the feelings and thoughts arising in themselves and others, modify their persona, and act again without any encouragement. What we seek to encourage, however, is the methodical rehearsal of roles that emphasize the collective purposes of the troupe, acts that self-consciously grow through demands on self and peers toward demands on a larger society. The educational system does not serve the students' purposes now. They must learn to use the crawl spaces we make available to them to prepare for organized acts that will render that system unworkable, and compel change.

Education is never problematic; it is natural to us as a species that we help our young grow up into the society they actually live in. Everyone and everything assists. The privileged, without thinking, grow up to drive cars, eat well, have jobs, speak the dominant dialect, go to college, participate in the political system, and expect that things will be managed for their convenience in most places they go. Of course, there are exceptions, but it is very difficult to imagine circumstances among the privileged that would fail to produce these general results. Their schools have little to do with it, except insofar as they reinforce the young people's idea that they are going to be relatively affluent, comfortable, and superior no matter what.

The children of the poor are also educated to grow up into the society they actually live in. Here, too, everything assists in preparing you for life: without having to reflect very much, you learn that food is not something you can count on, but that you will need to learn to cope with hunger and insecurity; you learn that many of the official practices around you won't make sense; you learn that following directions is generally safe, though boring, and carries no guarantee; that refusing to follow directions can have violent physical consequences or can leave you isolated and estranged; that many people will be suspicious of your motives, critical of how you express yourself, and doubtful about your abilities; that work will likely be dull and tedious; that authorities value your passivity much more than your intelligence; and you learn that joy will be largely associated with people and places hidden from formal authority, places where you feel comfortable, but that have little power over the larger world.

Schools for young people in poverty are marvelously successful at teaching about the scarcity of resources, arbitrariness of authority, and shunting of joy to peripheries that characterize the society they are actually growing up into. As a species, we hardly need to go out of our way at all to make sure that each caste develops the skills and abilities they will need to perform their caste function. It is merely human to help the young grow up this way.

What is difficult is helping the young grow up into a society that does not yet exist. For this problem, imagination and creativity are required, and there are many opponents to the attempt. We must act as we would if the young were growing up into a different society, not this one. Acting methodically in such a way means creating a small society that makes sense to grow up in with its own terms, collaborative norms, and cooperative ways. This is the underlying motivation of the small schools and charter schools movement (the part of the charter school movement, at least, that has not been corporatized): to generate settings where enough can be controlled that a small but healthy culture develops to ground and root the young in their tumultuous world. The Algebra Project classroom is another version of these mini-societies, designed as a healing, self-replicating "virus" within the ill body of an existing school.

Within this small society, education is again unproblematic. The democratic, challenging, inclusive, loud, but self-healing America that does not yet exist comes into existence within the terms of our play. And the development of persona, roles, acts, and total assertions that occurs within our play is both "imaginary" and real, just as the effects of a play in the theater or of a religious ritual are real. People change through action, and through encountering reaction, and through reflecting on the effects of what they have done. The fact that their actions take place in a self-consciously protected context, does not make their actions any less real. In fact, their actions in these contexts are *more* real, because they are performed in a state of heightened awareness, as opposed to the hum-drum of a deadened routine.

In any good class, the students feel alive in a way they do not feel when the class is bad. In an Algebra Project class, the students, mentors, and adults often feel startled, surprised at their own confidence and boldness. In the ordinary world, the principal is immensely powerful to the students' eye, symbolically elevated by rung after rung of authority. Mocking the principal, common among students, is funny because of the contrast between their august status and their common humanity—that their ears are too big or their voice squeaky or their clothes odd-looking. But to Algebra Project students, the principal may simply be an organizing target; we want the principal to extend our lunch period from thirty minutes to an hour and we refuse to accept that the person called "Principal Farmer" controls the length of the lunch period (her power is not that great), but *we* control the length of the lunch period and we will figure out how to get it extended. This way of thinking is arrogant, and it startles us when we realize that it is normal in our classroom, normal in the terms of our play.

When we are other places in the school or city and speak as we do in our play, people often seem to take offense. But we bring that observation back into the crawl space and work out different ways to incorporate the problem into our action so we can move the plot along. Story after story from the Civil Rights Movement reports this dynamic. "Don't call me 'boy.' My name's Mr. Steptoe," or even simply, "I am here to register to vote," are examples of language transferred from the crawl space—where acts of public courage were prepared—to a wider, more open stage. In the crawl space, among the people learning to struggle together, being called "Mr. Steptoe" or expressing the desire to vote were rich symbols referring in complicated ways to what we wanted to do and become. But used by a sharecropper on the streets of the Delta or lining up at the courthouse, those same words felt like weapons to white people who were not yet ready for their reality to change.

Ellison's novel is centered on this same question: How to prepare a dramatistic language, a language that can be used in action, so that those actions will rearrange the action of others and in fact change whole plots. At the beginning of *Invisible Man* this problem is represented by the narrator's encounter with a "tall, blond man," who bumps into the narrator, calls him "an insulting name," and curses him. The narrator, demanding an apology he doesn't get, beats the white man, almost kills him, and leaves him moaning and bleeding on the sidewalk, but then realizes he was invisible to the man as black people are, generally, to white people in America. It is not that white people see nothing, but what we see is largely an image from inside our own minds: "Then I was amused. Something in this man's thick head had sprung out and beaten him within an inch of his life." The book begins with this act of violence, but books are the actions of word-men and word-women, and the narrator finds himself at the end of the novel in "a hole in a basement" that he has filled, so far, with 1,369 light bulbs, the power lighting them up stolen from the electric company, an "act of sabotage, you know." He says that he is "hibernating" and that "hibernation is a covert preparation for a more overt action." Our Algebra Project classroom is just such a crawl space, a hole in the ground or fox-hole, of covert preparation for more overt action.

On January 17, 2009, at a bus stop, returning from work with the Algebra Project's peer tutoring site, Zachary Hallback, 19, was murdered by a young man trying to rob him. Algebra Project students had been organizing a "die-in" at the state capitol to press the Governor and State Legislature to comply with court orders requiring hundreds of millions of dollars in additional funding for Baltimore public schools. After the murder they named the action CSI Annapolis and demonstrated in Zach's memory.

TREY [*leading the chant in front of student marchers*]: No Education, No WHAT?!

MARCHERS [*responding*]: No Education, No Life!

TREY: No Education, No WHAT?!

MARCHERS: No Education, No Life!

TREY: No Education, No WHAT?!

MARCHERS: No Education, No Life!

CHRIS [*addressing the students through a bullhorn*]: We are here at the Governor's State House and Mansion because this is a crime scene. This is a crime scene because children are dying. Without high quality education, children die. The law requires more money for education, but Governor Martin O'Malley is wanted for

murder because he refuses to comply with
court orders.

RYAN [*taking his turn on the bullhorn*]: Zach
didn't have to die. But I feel sorry
for the brother that killed him, too. He
probably didn't have a proper education
or a proper job.

MARYLAND [*to herself*]: We have to be able to
love the killer, too.[17]

One of the scenes of instruction for the idealized Algebra Project classroom is the street demonstration, the
gathering of citizens to discuss the pressing issues of the
day, questioning rulers and challenging them to change.
It is a traditional scene in classical drama because the
relation of the people to authority is a political question
that each generation and polity must solve for itself.
Thinking of the street demonstration as an extension
of the drama of the classroom helps the young people
fashion their insurgency. Many people, old and young,
become frustrated with what is sometimes referred to as
"protest politics." Marches and demonstrations are often
blunt instruments, seem to accomplish little in the way
of practical change, and may lead to bad dialogue or no
dialogue, rather than to the consciousness raising dialec-
tic we seek.

But the Algebra Project's pedagogical process deliberately situates street demonstrations within the context
of "crawl space." We are not in the stage of full-blown
revolution, insurrection, or civil war. Insurgencies must

---

17 A video of the action on which this scene is based can
be found at http://www.youtube.com/watch?v=aSRgIs
ECnvE.

be earned through the patient laying up of stores till the people—or a large part of the people—achieve a new vision of what might be. We do not anticipate that rallies, protests, sit-ins, and marches will overthrow the government. What we anticipate is rather that the terminology the students use to size up their situation will change as they reflect on new experiences. That change in terminology provokes new acts, and those acts entail reactions that make room for the drama to be advanced. This is simply the method of the class extended to the street or to the school board meeting or to the courtroom, or to other settings that the students decide to engage, until the educational business-as-usual falls apart.

There are impediments, however, to this kind of extension of the classroom, just as there were impediments to the student activism of the Civil Rights Movement. It was important, as we discussed above, that the 1957 Civil Rights Act allowed the federal Department of Justice to "turn the key" and let the students out when the racist police were continually locking them up.

The Algebra Project constructs its crawl space specifically by doing math. Authorities are no more comfortable with domestic insurgents than they have ever been. Principals and school boards do not like "troublemakers." Left-wing or Africanist activists are still infiltrated, raided, and wiretapped as before. But all the educational and political authorities claim to be in love with science and math. Though they don't expect very much, they are even happy to throw money at math classrooms for poor children—not much money, but some. They believe they understand the significance of math and science education in the technological era, and they are willing to say they support mathematics for all.

The Algebra Project hides beneath the cover of this pro-mathematical orthodoxy. The students do not even need to mince words. They are like the purloined letter, hidden in plain sight. In pursuing their insurgency they disrupt the state capitol or a school board meeting, but go back to teaching their peers math, and so generally get left alone. Some school board members are even afraid that the students will ask them to solve an algebra problem or prove a theorem, and then the board's own cover as educated people would be blown. Math hides the student insurgency while it learns how to walk.

The most direct evidence for this claim is that the Algebra Project is an economically viable concern. Authorities with access to some cash are actually willing to sign it over to the students in exchange for their academic contribution to the mathematical education of their peers. And in fact, the students in Baltimore have earned more than $2 million over ten years sharing math knowledge in this way.

TWAN [*to DARIUS*]: Could you help Lucas with seeing how a cubic function can model the relation of the height of a box to its volume? [*Turning to Shontrice*] How is Malcolm doing with that?

SHONTRICE: He understands that the volume is the length times the width times the height. But he doesn't understand how to make an equation to show the functional relationship of the height to the volume.

TWAN: What questions can you ask to help him with that?

SHONTRICE: I could maybe ask him how we

could make different size boxes from the
same sheet of cardboard?
TWAN: Try it.

The students over some years have constructed a ladder
of peer teaching. Twan is in college majoring in math, but
teaches in the Algebra Project classroom in the afternoon.
He learned certain pedagogical techniques from X and
Sunshine, who graduated high school several years ago,
and from Mr. Jay, who teaches with him in the classroom.
These pedagogical techniques begin with doing something (like building a box from cardboard, taking a trip
on a bus, running a race, or playing a game), then move to
individual and collective reflection on what was done, then
to some kind of abstraction or refinement of terms, and
then to doing something that makes use of the new terms,
then reflecting again, abstracting again, reapplying, and so
on. The teacher's role is largely (1) to ensure that students
do things together that are physically distinctive enough
to constitute a common experience that can then be discussed and "mathematized," and (2) to ask questions that
will elicit verbal and symbolic acts from the students—
ideas that they can try out, experiment with, seek evidence
for, argue about, and eventually use to go further.

The similarity of this pedagogical technique and the
dramatistic process we have described above is, of course,
not accidental. The Algebra Project sees both the social
arrangements of a people and their mathematics not as
"givens," but rather as created things that have grown up
through the effect of human acts on the nonhuman scene
and on other human actors. Human societies and mathematics as a human activity grow through the development of language that encodes the shared experiences

of a people. Neither cultural practices nor mathematical ideas are fixed by higher authority. We say that the co-operative ways of a society—including its mathematical ideas—arise out of the common ground of human experience through the cycle of action, being affected by the world's reaction, and adopting revised roles and terminology in preparation for new action.

In the first two-thirds of the nineteenth century, slaves' acts of running away from bondage forced open opportunities to conceive and bring into being a country without slavery. In the 1950s and '60s, the impatient, organized demands of young people forced open opportunities to conceive and try to bring into being a country without segregated public accommodations and without segregated castes of voters and non-voters. In the twenty-first century, the dramatic rehearsals of young people in poverty teaching each other—building languages out of their common humanity to create their own mathematics, science, history, poetry, music, art, film, drama, and politics—will force open opportunities to extricate education from the caste system. This new insurgency will have to be even more seriously earned and more disruptive than the nation's turmoil in the 1960s, because this time the prize is not merely eating at a lunch counter, riding on a bus, or even voting. This time, the prize will be a social, political, and educational arrangement that does not permit one caste to exclude the children of another caste from the common good.

Part IV

Courtship and Pastoral[1]

I sang of quiet Achille, Afolabe's son,
who never ascended in an elevator,
who had no passport, since the horizon needs none,

never begged nor borrowed, was nobody's waiter,
whose end, when it comes, will be a death by water
(which is not for this book, which will remain unknown

and unread by him). I sang the only slaughter
that brought him delight, and that from necessity—
of fish, sang the channels of his back in the sun.

I sang our wide country, the Caribbean Sea.
Who hated shoes, whose soles were as cracked as a stone,
who was gentle with ropes, who had one suit alone,

whom no man dared insult and who insulted no one,
whose grin was a white breaker cresting, but whose
frown was a growing thunderhead, whose fist of iron

would do me a greater honour if it held on
to my casket's oarlocks than mine lifting his own
when both anchors are lowered in the one island.

—Derek Walcott, *Omeros*, (LXIV.1)

---

1   My use of the terms "courtship" and "pastoral" comes from
     Burke's *Rhetoric of Motives*, 208ff. and 123ff.

What remains for this book is a description of the tools
or techniques that we will need in order to develop a consensus among the many different kinds of people who
must coalesce into a shared insurgency. This is not a small
problem. Our focus has been on the young descendants
of slaves; but the project of developing an education insurgency, though led by young people, will need places
and roles for many different identities and many different
kinds of identification. There is an open question about
how an uprising from below will be organized and about
the symbols, images, metaphors, and terms that will name
and shape a common act. This chapter describes an approach to finding such symbols, terms, and ways of communicating in and around schools of poverty.

Building alliances between and among young people
and adults will require pragmatic ways of relating to each
other that are generally considered strange in schools.
Trapped in the middle of all the other social institutions
that oppress young people, schools almost automatically
provoke alienation and either passive or active hostili-
ty, as we have seen. An important reason for this normal dynamic is that virtually all adults in schools feel
responsible for the orderliness of the institution and are
convinced that without adult control, disorder will result.
This sense of responsibility and conviction is mirrored
by the young people, who have learned their lessons well
and believe that adult control is necessary to keep them
from wildness. Most young people are certain that this is
true at least of their peers, though many exempt themselves from the general rule.

In any case, this picture of the relation between adult
control and young people's wildness is a disaster for education in schools of poverty. Starting from such a simplistic

premise ensures that common purposes will be elusive. Wealthier schools are run on the same premise, but most young people in those schools accept the adult purpose of reproducing bourgeois values and relationships, because those values and relationships seem to satisfy most of their needs and desires. They comply. In schools of poverty, what is reproduced is poverty and oppression; the needs of young people are not met. They resist.

We have to do away with the idea that young people will be wild without adult control and coercion, but that means that we also have to find ways to teach and develop an alternative relationship. Older adults and teachers can't simply let go and see what happens. Simply letting go means that the normal forces in the society sweep in and nothing changes. The idealized Algebra Project classroom described in Part III doesn't just happen; it is to some extent the consequence of a plan. What plan?

> Knowledge, learning, technological power, conditioning and the like…All such scientific approaches have great admonitory value. They provide us with incongruous perspectives that allow us to see mankind from many angles, each of which in its way adds a new "hark ye" to the lore of human relations. But they are all extrinsic, non-substantial approaches—and as such are not suited to define man's essential dramatic nature. They heckle so superbly that many in the audience come to mistake the heckling for the address.[2]

A dramatistic approach suggests that the roles of young people in schools of poverty should be considered much more carefully. Perhaps the principal players are not

---

2   Burke, *A Grammar of Motives*, 252.

the teachers imparting knowledge, but the students trying
to live and thrive. It is their address that we older people
as audience or as secondary characters must attempt to
interpret and to allow ourselves to be affected by. Maybe
the teachers' and authorities' knowledge and learning and
technological power and conditioning are so much heck-
ling, extrinsic to the real drama, distracting us from what
the players are attempting to represent and enact.

The students' concern is not primarily knowledge,
learning, or technological power, although those things
do promise important perspectives. Their concern is primarily the creation of life, creation perfectly appropriate
to adolescence. They are attempting to make a way for
themselves, and as they make a way, to form themselves
in conformity to a democratic, egalitarian society that
does not yet exist. In fact, the hoped-for democratic and
egalitarian society is very concrete and immediate for
them, because they are moving from the class of youth
into the class of adults, becoming equal to that higher
class, leveling the difference with each passing year.

We have been recommending the rehearsal of a stage
drama as a representative anecdote for understanding
this attempt. And we have encouraged attention to the
way the young people must simultaneously address three
audiences: themselves in their interior dialogue; their
peers or co-players on stage; and a wider audience beyond the scene of rehearsal. Our idealized Algebra Project classroom protects a crawl space where these forms
of address may be tried out and practiced without the
constant threat of rupture and disintegration, and despite
the real brittleness of the spaces the students live in that
are less protected. The example of the classroom is intended to show that the work of performing the drama

must be done primarily by the young themselves, not by adults. So the first part of the plan involves perceiving the students as the principal actors, the center of the action—not the adults, and not the curriculum.

This requires a degree of humility on the part of teachers in particular. We teachers tend to think of ourselves as dominant in some way, creating the classroom culture and mood, setting goals, evaluating, and so on. After all, we know more about the subject being taught; we are significant. But it doesn't therefore follow that we are central. We may start from the contemporary dictum about the teacher's role—"Not the sage on the stage, but the guide at the side"—and push it a little further by asking: "What *is* our role on the stage, given that we share it with the young people, and given that they are the principal actors?"

The essential difficulty here is that we enter into the dramatic relation of the school or classroom encumbered by the frozen, unhelpful social categories that pit the young people's wildness against adult control. Those categories or hierarchies of, at least, "teacher" vs. "student," "adult" vs. "youth," credentialed vs. not-yet-credentialed are so pervasively established that they give the starting-point of the interaction. So the second part of our plan involves acknowledging that these complex and in many ways debilitating hierarchies cannot simply be ignored. To create new relationships or roles in the educational drama will require some movement or plot development that takes us from a problematic initial state of possibly contradictory purposes within established hierarchies to a new state of something more like harmony and consensus.

One way to approach this movement or plot development is by looking at traditional cultural forms that deal with communication or negotiation between different kinds or classes in society. An example of such a form is courtship between two people, and it turns out that rituals of courtship have obvious parallels to negotiations or communication between other paired "kinds." I am suggesting that courtship can be used to model the interactions of teachers and students who are seeking common purposes.

This is a handy topic, since maybe not the word, but certainly the practice of courtship is on the young people's minds. Instinctively, they understand the first step in negotiating romantic differences. They understand because they are symbol users. The first step must acknowledge the mystery that courtship is a kind of communication between different beings who are necessarily the same in some ways, but distinct in others: they are beings of the same kind and of different kinds. And because of this difference there is necessarily some mystery or strangeness between them that requires acknowledgement. Lucas acknowledges this mystery by playfully hitting Chantel, whom he likes. G.P. shouts cuss-words and insults at Shontrice who delightedly cusses back. Malcolm flirts by hovering nearby and throwing things. Kayla sends text messages about Jasmine. The first step cannot be direct. There is no such thing in symbol-using. The first step in this most intimate form of address is to create an obstacle, an indirection. The symbolic creation of an obstacle acknowledges the mystery of communication between different kinds.

In the creative work that young people must do, there are many, many different kinds to accommodate beyond male and female. Social hierarchies are well-established in the brittle world between black and other "races," men and women, gay and straight, rich and poor, teacher and student, parent and child. These classes are building blocks for entire structures of much more complicated hierarchies that go well beyond binary oppositions.

In all these different structures, communication between kinds is initiated through the symbolic positioning of obstacles essential to courtship: standoffishess, reticence, indirection, allusion, formalisms of all sorts. And the actions of young people in schools can be interpreted in this way. Their obstinacy, their reluctance, their difficult, challenging adolescent acts may be seen as elements of courtship designed as first steps toward harmonizing the hierarchies that will otherwise limit or oppress them. The literal-minded, of course, just see reluctance as reluctance and a challenge to authority as a challenge to authority. But these interpretations underestimate the subtlety of the young students. An actress's reluctance on stage may be a way to represent her hidden desire; bravado on stage may represent a complex fear. Why not express the "true" emotions directly? From the actor's perspective, there are many possible reasons: the character may not be fully conscious of the "true" emotions or may not understand them or may be ashamed of them. Or one character may be unsure how another character will respond to their actual feelings, and so must present a test in an indirect form.

The third part of our plan for arriving at a consensus is therefore to recognize explicitly that students in school, and especially students in poverty, fit these delicate patterns of courting, and to respond with appropriate decorum. They do not fully understand themselves and are often ashamed of or embarrassed by their thoughts and feelings. Nor are they confident of how others, peers or adults, will react to them and so they send out all kinds of

confusing signals. These are obvious facts about adolescents. But we are too quick to write this kind of thing off
as "immaturity." We understand actors on stage who do
similar things as attempting to negotiate complicated social relations. Why do we think the complexity of social
relations faced by adolescents is any easier to negotiate?
As we have seen, young people in schools of poverty and
their teachers experience the whole weight of America's
social and political history bearing down on them. And
we have also seen that there is virtually no room in these
schools for students to make their own thoughts and
feelings heard, or for them to make much sense of what
they are hearing in return from adults.

No one doubts that adolescents are theatrical: they are
too angry, too sullen, too boisterous; they laugh too much;
they cry too much. But theater is never to be interpreted
literally. It is symbolic action. It entails much more than
is shown on the surface. From one point of view we are
simply emphasizing what developmental psychologists
and good parents or teachers already know. But from another point of view, we are discussing not the psychology
of adolescents, but their implicit politics. The dramatic
stance that seems to indicate their isolation and aloofness
can also be read as opening themselves symbolically to
the possibility of alliances and shared action. They address
themselves to this monumental problem with very little
help. But they are persistent. In the midst of our current
social organization designed under the flag of property,
war, and competition, their many forms of exaggeration
may conceal complex social motives, as you would guess
if you saw them acting the same way on a stage.

Gestures, tokens, songs, dances, words. Courtship is
made up of a to-ing and fro-ing between beings that are

in many ways alike and in some important ways different. There is, of course, romantic courtship. But there is
also the courtliness required by the social or political differences in status that arise necessarily in the presence of
the king or queen or president or principal or any other
authority. There is the forensic formality or courtliness
that is automatically generated by the elevation of a mag-
istrate who must symbolically be wooed. Though men of
a certain class may still stand when a woman enters the
room, everyone of all classes rises for a judge. Whenever
one must be careful of how one speaks or acts in order to
procure the favor of another who has power to confer or
deny, courtship may be involved.

In the past, it seemed obvious that students sought
the teacher's favor, and were careful how they acted and
how they spoke so that they could obtain the advance-
ments that it was in the teacher's power to confer. But
today, things are not so simple: teachers and authorities
must also court the young people's favor, and must be
careful, too, how they speak and act. Differences in status, class, and kind provoke uncertainties about how others will respond to us; thrown together, we must decide
how to communicate despite these uncertainties. The
typical schools have mostly abandoned the attempt and
simply accept the actual failure or impossibility of communication between kinds. Rather than the harmonies
and insights of successful communication, these schools
reproduce what is called a "permanent underclass," that
is, a class permanently forced and coerced, or jilted and
abandoned in a parody of courtship.

But we are imagining the flowering of communication between kinds, when the drama, ritual, and dance
might build to a unity of purpose despite the necessary

mysteries and uncertainties. There can be no doubt that the purposes of student and teacher, or of youth and authority *begin* as partially distinct. The drama and dance is to bring those distinctions into harmony so that they may amount to a shared purpose.

And the goal for a radical approach to education is not merely a feeling or emotion, or even a union between the students and teachers, or a union among the students themselves. These are only intermediate means towards the larger end of fashioning an insurgency involving millions of people, young and old. The idealized Algebra Project classroom is a representative anecdote preparing a stance or attitude that befits insurgents in a democracy. Young people in poverty push us towards this stance by eluding all rules, initiatives, and false curricula; we have been shamefully simple, awkward, and clumsy with them. An increase in sophistication on our part, much better readings of the students' intentions and desires, is an important step in recognizing consensus and shared purposes. They will dance more elegantly when we make better partners.

The next step in our plan for harmonizing the purposes of younger and older people in schools is in a way somewhat technical. It involves some nuances about hierarchical relations that are usually only implicit, and that rarely surface in our awareness. I would like to discuss these nuances by an excursion into the literary genre of pastoral, the genre that explores courtship between people of different statuses in society. Pastoral literature traditionally uses an idealized society of shepherds or farmers as a device for exploring social, political, ethical, or aesthetic questions. The key element is that some topic or concern of a "sophisticated" group or class gets treated or addressed by a more "simple" class. So shepherds might discuss the proper way to govern a kingdom or woo a maiden in verse. Though shepherds and farmers are normal in the pastoral tradition, there are infinite variations. Fables involving animals, common to most cultures, are one example: human concerns are addressed in a purportedly simplified way by "lower" animals. The Western genre in film is another example with its own sub-varieties: Easterners are thrown into the world of less "sophisticated" cowboys, or white settlers come into contact with "less civilized" natives or Mexicans. Science fiction novels and films also use pastoral structures when an extra-terrestrial or futuristic civilization represents the "simple life" or some kind of primitivism in contrast to a more complex or exhausted civilization. No matter the variation, pastoral always involves one subset of society that is positioned as simple, relatively primitive, closer to nature or to uncorrupted human relations, and another subset of society that is, by contrast, more complex, more formal, further from an imagined "original" state, and more corrupt. This basic contrast is varied by shadings of all kinds, mostly because the audiences of the pastoral mode are almost always members of the more sophisticated or corrupt class.

For William Empson the virtue of the pastoral genre is that it allows consideration of class differences without denying either the strengths or the weaknesses of any party. "The essential trick of the old pastoral, which was felt to imply a beautiful relation between rich and poor," he writes, "was to make simple people express strong feelings (felt as the universal subject, something fundamentally true about everybody) in learned and fashionable language (so that you wrote about the best subject in the best way)."[3] In pastoral, there is a "clash between style and theme," because the theme insists that the shepherds are wise and the courtiers have something to learn from them, while the style is by and for the upper classes.

But the inadequacy of the purportedly sophisticated people "implies the tone of humility normal to pastoral." "So 'fundamentally true' goes to 'true about people in all parts of society, even those you wouldn't expect.' 'I now abandon my specialized feelings [for example, of class, race, gender, or nationality] because I am trying to find better ones.'"[4] It is interesting to note that Empson believed *Alice in Wonderland* marked an important development in the pastoral genre. *Alice* inaugurated the use of adults and children as a courting pair: adults are sophisticated and corrupted; children pretend to be simple and untainted; but each needs ways to understand and influence the other, and both are powerful in their own right.

Baltimore's world-famous T.V. show, *The Wire*, has many of these pastoral ingredients and is useful to consider in the respect that it is not quite what we are looking for. There is certainly an implied wisdom in many of the working class characters: drug dealers, grandmothers, students, dock workers. And the sophisticated characters are frequently or even usually humbled. But to the extent that the show is intended to be or is actually taken as a depiction of reality, we have moved away from the purposes of pastoral towards some other purposes. The danger, as with naturalistic narrative generally, is that audiences come to believe that they "know" the characters, settings, motives, and so on of the people represented.

---

3   William Empson, *Some Versions of Pastoral* (New York: New Directions, 1974), 11.

4   Ibid., 19.

In the pastoral tradition that we are promoting, there is a self-conscious but, as Empson says, "tactfully unmentioned" irreality, a clash between the style and subject. Shepherds are not noblemen, but as equal characters in the drama, they may be able to express truths about people in all parts of society, truths the nobility themselves might have difficulty expressing. Shakespeare's clowns, fools, and laborers, or the outlandish aliens or robots in science fiction, for example, often play this role, exposing the folly or hypocrisy of the upper classes through their undercutting, unmasking wit. The effect, however, is not naturalistic. There is no pretense that the lives of the poor in Shakespeare are thoroughly represented, because the clash between style and subject is intentionally too great. The purpose rather of representing shepherds and fools is "to attempt to reconcile some conflict between the parts of a society" (p. 19), conflicts that to some extent parallel conflicts within individual selves.

This is an important distinction for our argument because we are trying to understand young people as *doing* something in schools that goes well beyond the acquisition of knowledge. If school were only about learning and knowledge, then accurate observation of schools could settle for literal descriptions of reality, as *The Wire* is taken to be. But we see young people in schools as trying to establish forms of life that satisfy their own human and political interests, including developing alliances both among themselves and with the world of older adults. No literal description could possibly represent this purpose, because the young people's acts or purpose cannot be "observed" or "depicted": you literally cannot *see* what young people are doing in schools; you can only *interpret* what they are doing from the surface that you see, and then re-act for your own purposes. Your interpretation is bound to be wrong and your response unhelpful if you are using an inadequate frame.

The unreality of the representation, the weakening of the naturalistic motive, and the obvious formality of address are what make pastoral appropriate to the study of young people in schools, just as it made pastoral appropriate over centuries to the study of courtship. Courtship between lovers, between black and white, rich and poor, young and old, urban and rural, requires the conscious placing of an obstacle or distorting lens as the first step, not the pretense of transparent windows onto the other. Awkwardness, a degree of opacity or mystery, is inevitable. Similarly, teachers and students must come to understand that we are doing something much more difficult and indirect than merely "communicating knowledge": we are trying to find a way of relating to each other as equals with shared purposes despite all the obstacles in our way. And to do this we must start by adding some obstacles of our own making, because that is how human societies have always gone about bridging the differences between classes, genders, and castes. We include an awareness of the pastoral structure of classrooms and schools in our plan, because we need ways to help the "sophisticated" teachers act more humbly without giving up their strengths, and we need ways to help the students see themselves as able and even in some senses dominant, while remembering that they are not yet fully formed.

It is hard to imagine, for example, that watching *The Wire* is actually a very good form of preparation for teachers who are about to begin teaching in Baltimore's segregated schools. They would be better off reading *King Lear* or *As You Like It*—plays with important pastoral elements—or even attempting performances of them. This is because the preparation required is not knowledge or information about what Baltimore is "really" like, but a stance in relation to the students' stances or to the administrators', a readiness to act in the physical presence of other people and to be affected by their reactions.

We invent formalisms and styles of all sorts, "self-interferences" Burke calls them, in order to find the right posture and tone for doing what we want. We teach young children not simply to take or grab, but to impose a restraint on themselves, to wait their turn, to say "please" and "thank you." The social requirement has nothing to do with physical constraints. There may be plenty of cookies to go around, but we still want our children to ask for them politely. Courtesy (from the same etymology as "courtship") is a human invention responding to the rhetorical conditions of being in the presence of another human being; we impose the resistances of politeness on ourselves because such formalism, or self-interference, is rhetorically persuasive, induces action in beings who by nature respond to symbols, and fits with the ethics and aesthetics of our people.

Bob Moses refers to this practice of self-interference as "straight-jacketing," with the provision that the straight-jackets are self-imposed by an individual or a group of peers as opposed to the straight-jacketing imposed by a superior on a subordinate.[5] "Straight-jacketing" describes the formal mechanisms underlying demands on oneself and one's peers. The young people of the Baltimore Algebra Project have evolved a complicated internal culture, governed by both implicit and explicit rules, that helps them achieve the purposes they have worked out

5   Moses and Cobb, *Radical Equations*, 198.

for themselves. Not any old straight-jacket will do. Many are possible, but only some advance the work. The young people themselves must figure out what formal structure of the classroom or of their meeting space will hold them tight but still let them move enough to get things done. In a play, you conform to the straight-jacket of your lines, but wriggle around until you can speak and act within the constraints of the script to express the full freedom of your own being. And the students must figure out how to speak and listen to each other as well as to their teachers so that they can succeed both in learning academically and in representing their views on how schools and society need to change.[6]

At the same time, teachers, parents, and organizers must develop an appreciation for this labor of the

---

6   "Straight-jacketing" also refers in the Algebra Project to the strategy used by mathematicians and scientists to structure language for specific purposes, because both political and mathematical work require consensus-building about the formalities to be used. Mathematics is a language expressly structured by communities of mathematicians. They come to agree, as a historical process, on ways to represent human experiences, thoughts, and expressions. And they have learned to be very strict with each other about how their representations are to be used and in what contexts, so that more work can get done. For example, taking the square root of a negative number is not permitted in the set of real numbers, but is permitted in the set of complex numbers. This finesse allows mathematicians to solve all kinds of theoretical problems, and allows scientists and engineers to solve all kinds of practical problems, even though there is nothing to point to—no physical referent for—"the square root of negative one." In both mathematics and politics, groups of people agree to use formal representations for symbolic purposes that go well beyond what are normally thought of as "literal" meanings. These representations, however, "get work done."

students, awkward as the students will often be. The young people will hit all kinds of wrong notes as they learn their roles individually and collectively; older people should understand that this awkwardness is normal in pastoral—not just a "phase," but rather the way any viable style actually evolves. The pastoral interaction between "sophisticated" and "simple" people necessarily produces a sense of awkwardness and misunderstanding or misrepresentation; either the simple sound pretentious or the sophisticated appear stiff. To the extent that pastoral is successful in stabilizing conflicts between parts of society, a new style develops that is neither all the one nor all the other.

Developing this new style within the shifting context of a complex hierarchical relationship is the next step in our plan. Our point is that straight-jackets or formalisms are devised to move us forward in what we are doing; they are chosen. Whether invented or discovered, they must be adopted by human actors for human purposes or they are useless. In schools, the young people are the players, and must come to devise—or at least to adapt—the straight-jackets that will allow their acts to succeed and their assertions to have force. Older people must encourage and support the attempt to find new formalisms, new styles, that will let the necessary work be accomplished. We are trying to make explicit and bring to consciousness the possibility that older people and younger people may be working toward shared goals even when things don't seem that way on the surface. Contests between the generations over speech and dress, for example, can be considered dramatistically as disagreements about the nature of the formalities appropriate to a given scene. The youth feels constrained by needing to pull his pants up and wear a belt in school. The elder points out that he is acting as if constrained by the "pressure" or conventions of his peers to let his pants hang down. Tristian is not the least bit embarrassed, has breached no decorum he acknowledges, to curse spectacularly in the middle of class. But he missed three days of school waiting for his hair to grow a certain amount after a barber did something that apparently made him unpresentable according to the refined standards of his age. Formalisms, signs, and insignia are everywhere, but their purposes vary with the actions they advance. To find common purposes, we must come to accept new formalities.

We are recommending an increase in the sophistication with which we view questions of stance and voice, breaches of decorum or taboo, and especially to understand the choice of more humble or nonconformist affectations as potentially pastoral strategies intended to bridge the gap between generations, classes, or genders, but indirectly and with style, as a version of courting, rather than hitting straight on. Ordinarily in schools, these things are thought of simply as violations. Students are rude, slovenly, or disobedient. But if we had greater appreciation of the social, political, and symbolic complexities involved, we might be better able to interpret the students' acts as advancing *collaborative* interests. The study of dramatic poetry is useful in this regard. Rehearsing the performance of lines like the following can help us prepare stances we might use ourselves or that we might recognize others using around us. Understanding "reality" often means understanding that someone is trying on a role. Once we start thinking about how role-playing works, we can adjust our responses to collaborate towards a shared purpose.

Edgar: ...My face I'll grime with filth,
   Blanket my loins, elf all my hair in knots,
   And with presented nakedness outface
   The winds and persecutions of the sky.
   The country gives me proof and precedent
   Of Bedlam beggars, who with roaring voices
   Strike in their numb'd and mortified bare arms
   Pins, wooden pricks, nails, sprigs of rosemary;
   ... [*Trying on a new voice*] Poor Turlygod! Poor Tom!
   That's something yet. Edgar I nothing am.
            (*King Lear*, II.3.9–21)

This is a banished, disinherited son seeking a strategy to be reconciled with his father. His straight-jacket is the disguise of a lunatic. Edgar's father, the Lord of Gloucester, misjudged him, interpreted his actions using too narrow a frame, and now the son is courting his father's favor, but with wild indirection: by pretending to be a Bedlam beggar. Edgar changes and debases himself in accordance with the trick of pastoral to occupy a low place as a method of indirection for finding common ground with something higher. He is in the predicament of an adolescent trying on a new role. His piercings and histrionics, and later in the play his outlandish jargon, are theatrical, but not at all indiscriminate or "oppositional," as they would now be called. Rather, he seeks out the lowest places in order to gain access and keep proximity to the king and to his father, noting their reactions and developing a fuller way of life as he educates himself through his affections. We tend to think of a certain kind of adolescent dress and speech as rebellion, but what if we thought of the same dress and speech as a disguise, designed to distract attention from the underlying motives, not of rebellion, but of a desire to conform to substance rather than to surfaces.

Disguised in this way, Edgar begins serving his father as a guide and helper, though Gloucester's misfortune only grows and grows. Nevertheless, this service slowly advances the hoped-for reconciliation.

Gloucester: [*his eyes now gouged out by the villains, but guided in his blindness by the disguised Edgar, who still pretends to be Poor Tom O'Bedlam.*]
    Methinks thy voice is alter'd and thou speak'st
    In better phrases and matter than thou didst.
Edgar: You're much deceiv'd. In nothing am I changed
    But in my garments.
Gloucester: Methinks y'are better spoken.

Where some healing or alliance is occurring through a dramatic ritual, social division or ranks are neither fixed nor unchanging. From the brutal perspective of property, war, and competition, ranks or hierarchies are either static or suddenly inverted, where for example the rich fear that the poor, unchained, will murder them all, or that students, given "freedom," will overrun their schools. But under the sign of courtship, initiated by self-interference or other straight-jacketing formalisms willingly put on, differences in status are necessary starting points for finding new terms or principles that move us toward a shared purpose. To do this, we must be open to new patterns or styles of relationship that may not always match our preconceptions, just as Gloucester could not have foreseen his son Edgar needing to disguise himself.

We should not imagine that our students are consigned to a permanent status at the bottom, no matter how undeveloped they may initially appear. Nor are we interested in rewarding the simple reversal of the established order, those "successes" whereby the once destitute student becomes a tycoon, general, or surgeon. Instead, we attempt through deliberate demands on ourselves and on our peers, through purposeful formalisms, to throw the common principle of a humane and better ordering into relief, so that we and they may participate on many levels simultaneously. The young people are both ignorant *and* knowing. The teachers are both authoritative *and* deferential to the students. Rather than judge, we look for an interpretation of the young people's acts that lets us see their purposes as converging with ours. Their status is low, but we use the pastoral trick of showing how the lowest ranks share in the mystery and power of the highest, once order is based on common principles and shared purposes. The alternative view is that status is fixed and depends on arbitrary impositions of naked force—the "absolute" authority of adults, or the ultimate authority of the police to exclude "rebellious" young people from schools and communities. We reject that alternative.

Dramatic rituals are realistic and pragmatic; they perform work that makes things different. A classroom conceived in this way performs the work of binding the young to their own selves, to each other, and to a world outside. What opens is a series of ascents, a joyous elevation. The mystifications of educated vs. ignorant, or teacher vs. student, or higher status vs. lower status, or wealth vs. poverty, or white vs. black, or black vs. white, are still powerful, but lose their power to exclude and isolate us. Just as in a play, characters who represent opposing principles can collaborate to build a meaning beyond either principle taken separately, so the distinctions of class or status can themselves become common goods. Through our ritual discipline of self-interference and affection, they no longer appear as obstacles, but become our people's wealth and treasure. The students are not controlled by the society's dialectics or by their relationships to authority, but explore and use them for their own purposes.

Rosalind: [*disguised as a shepherd-boy named Ganymede*] Love is merely a madness, and, I tell you, deserves as well a dark house and a whip as madmen do; and the reason why they are not so punished and cured is, that the lunacy is so ordinary that the whippers are in love too. Yet I profess curing it by counsel.

Orlando: Did you ever cure any so?

Rosalind: Yes, one; and in this manner. He was to imagine me his love, his mistress; and I set him every day to woo me: at which time would I, being but a moonish youth, grieve, be effeminate, changeable, longing and liking; proud, fantastical, apish, shallow, inconstant, full of tears, full of smiles, for every passion something, and for no passion truly anything, as boys and women are, for the most part, cattle of this colour; would now like him, now loathe him; then entertain him, then forswear him; now weep for him, then spit at him; that I drave my suitor from his mad humour of love to a living humour of madness, which was, to forswear the full stream of the world, and to live in a nook merely monastic. And thus I cured him; and this way will I take upon me to wash your liver as clean as a sound sheep's heart, that there shall not be one spot of love in't.

Orlando: I would not be cured, youth.

Rosalind: [more gently]: I would cure you, if you would
but call me Rosalind, and come every day to my cote
and woo me.

Orlando: Now, by the faith of my love, I will.

(*As You Like It*, III.ii)

Rosalind, disguised as a boy, tells the boy she loves
(who in fact loves her) that he should pretend she is
herself, so that she can toy with his emotions and drive
him out of love. He first refuses, then agrees—all so they
can find a way to acknowledge their shared purpose.
Our students, pretending they don't care about learning,
though they really do, tell us, their teachers (who in fact
love them and believe in them), that we should pretend
they *do* care, so that they can toy with our emotions until,
after we have become nearly hopeless, they finally agree
to learn.

Our classrooms are rehearsals of this scene attempted over and over, and the only reason we don't understand how common it is, is that the lunacy is so ordinary.
Good teachers and all students, both, come to school in
the madness of love and to be cured of it, which does
not mean to be rid of it, but to progress through our
play-acting, through trying out poses and costumes, the
straight-jacketing of lines and voices, to a purposeful vi-
tality from an aimless wildness. Education is a socializing
process, but a growth into limitless, inspired acts of representation, not a submission.

To see the students as anything other than desperately
in love and desperate to learn is the schools' worst error.
Birds fly; fish swim; people learn.[7] Learning is how we

---

7   I'm paraphrasing John Holt from his excellent book, *How
Children Learn* (New York: Da Capo, 1995).

survive and thrive, and is never avoided. Teachers or parents are always wrong to fall for the mask of disinterestedness. Young people are helpless with desire to be joined to the richness of adult life which they see shimmering ahead of them. In the broken and inadequate orderings that constitute present-day America, what shimmers seems to be the Babylonian luxuries: money, sex, cars, intoxication, fame, glamour in towers, and leisure by the sea. But glamour means a false magic, a mist. If we could help them invent a plausible alternative as the type of the desired life, the young people could practice their affection on more subtle and useful objects and be cured.

So the final step in our plan is to thoughtfully and consciously imagine and rehearse collective acts of invention in schools and everywhere young people are. The Babylonian mirage is built from the principle that there are winners and losers, and the students in our schools, by that principle, are likely to lose. But the alternative image of the desired life is built on the principle of the common good, a good that can only be found with great subtlety, adventure, and willingness to try out new roles. We will know the students are growing and evolving when we begin to see not brutal assertions or reversals of hierarchical orderings, not outright disrespect or competitive boasts, but symbolic inversions, willed self-interferences like Edgar's or Rosalind's. These take the form of new creations, inventions, art, music, films, plays, books that young people make and read, classes they teach for each other, political campaigns, clubs, new organizations, dances, trips that young people plan and execute for themselves, with older people's help and involvement as accepted. These creations constitute the charmed pastoral settings with their own formalities and conventions that allow young people to communicate with each other and with older people across boundaries for common purposes.

The undoing of the sign of property and war into the pastoral inversions of rich and poor, educated and uneducated, is the motive of our classroom. Our goal is to live under the sign of courting and peace. This takes practice. We are sometimes stilted and artificial, and there are many misunderstandings, as in any courtship. But our work rises to joy and to principled reversals that ennoble all the participants and audiences of the play.

But we are not celebrating or glorying in primitivism or ignorance or poverty; these are pastoral conceits, seeing the students as shepherds in love or as wandering Bedlam beggars. The analogies are useful to understand that the complications of the whole society are inherent in the simplicity of the students' lives, and so that the classroom is an appropriate stage for working out the rich and full life roles that the young people are desperate to develop.

Because, finally, why a mathematics classroom? Why not English or history or music? Those would do almost as well. But it was an unpredictable development in the species' history that just now in these difficult times the contest is between a conception of life heavily weighted towards technological and scientific advances on the one hand, and a conception of life that stresses unquantifiable hierarchies of humane values on the other.

We in the Algebra Project protect places for young people to fashion an insurgency that will destabilize the technocracy so that a series of values under the sign of peace and the people will hold more sway, undo the modern peonage of the educational system, inspire literacy of all kinds in those who previously were assigned to a caste of slaves, prisoners, cannon fodder, the uneducated, and the unemployed.

But in protecting these places for the fashioning of insurgency, we do not intend to be outflanked by a simplistic contrast between hard realities and soft idealisms. It is not naked coercion or simple reversals we seek. The democracy in which we practice, but that does not yet exist, requires something more significant. We seek literal power based on principled reversals, which may use, but do not need to crush opposing principles. The idea is not to destroy technology or deny the power it represents, but to understand technology as part of a graded series, a hierarchy of values, though neither as the top of the hierarchy nor as the principle on which the hierarchy is based. The principle upon which our hierarchy of values is based depends instead on the common good as worked out in the drama of our dealings with each other and with the world. Math, science, technology, efficiency, data, knowledge, money, property, have their roles to play as shaped and used by human beings. But they are not principles of democracy and equality. They are not substantial enough; they are not hard enough. Mathematics and the hard sciences do their work; we respect their beauty and power so deeply that we have committed ourselves to leading the young people through the steps of their intricate figures and forms. But the sciences must themselves be rooted in the even stronger ground of the common good that cannot be determined by knowledge alone, but that must rather be approached patiently through our imaginative and dramatic action. Who will have access to knowledge and how, is not a question to be settled once and for all, but is rather the ground of a dramatic contest that we are already engaged in. The action we seek must take no delight in the slaughter or waste of anybody's children, nor refuse consciousness of tragedy and history; we must allow ourselves to be affected by the desires and actions of young people in poverty, so that both we and they may act more gracefully, in more successful courtship.

So by the young people's demanding of themselves and succeeding in mastering their mathematics, with our help, they will demonstrate that the contest is not for the victory of one faction over another, the technocrats over the humanists, or the humanists over the technocrats. They will demonstrate that the victory is for the principled series that leads from our common experiences, through the challenges of formalisms of all kinds and of all peoples, through science and math and poetry and music and art, to active assertions of shared purpose and to the inversions of old terms and ways of living that yield creations of substance and even more life.

Some readers may have remarked that the authorities in this book are a little dated. Ella Baker, Ralph Ellison, Kenneth Burke, and William Empson had their heyday from the 1930s through the early 1960s, more than half a century ago, and Bob Moses was steeped in the intellectual atmosphere of that period. I have sought them out because they were masters of "covert preparation for more overt action." Even Bob Moses, who in many ways guided the very active activists of SNCC, was not someone who rushed to every demonstration or sit-in, but chose rather to spend his time doing the patient work of listening and talking to people, seeking grounds for consensus and strategies for moving the country forward.

One of the achievements of the 1960s and 1970s was in fact that preparation for insurgency or revolution could be *overt* and explicit in a way that was not previously possible. Black Studies departments in universities, for example, are great things partly because they allow talk about ideas that in the 1950s and 1960s might have gotten you black-listed, jailed, or shot. Now, with enough footnotes, discussion of the same ideas might get you tenure.

But in some ways this openness is not a boon. In some ways, "ethnic studies" are just white liberalism's way of tying up some loose ends. The overtness of talk about revolution might turn out to make revolution *less* likely, because insurrection has become just one more lifestyle or market niche. One of the best selling images on the internet is Che Guevara. Neoliberalism grants everyone space to do their thing as long as they don't interfere with the accumulation of capital. Consequently, there is no need to create crawl space. Just book a meeting room in the air conditioned student center, or write a blog.

Fortunately, though, "freedom" does not extend everywhere in the neoliberal world. It is still a foreign concept in schools of poverty. In our infernal schools, we are blessed with the opportunity of having to protect ourselves, because young people of color are still a little too dangerous to be riled up just any old way. The 2012 dismantling of the Chicano Studies program in Tucson Public Schools is a good example. The program was very successful academically. If it had been taught on a university campus, it would have been nothing out of the ordinary. But in a high school for Mexican Americans, teaching about oppression and revolution offended the white power structure. Something was being done in the open that apparently must still be confined to a crawl space. The program was shut down, the students dispersed, and the teachers reassigned.[1]

But this problem is actually a blessing because it requires us to invent a new discipline and formalism, a set of new straight-jackets, a sufficient style, that will let us

---

1   Both Paolo Friere's *Pedagogy of the Oppressed* and William Shakespeare's *The Tempest* were banned by the Tucson school board. Chicano youth, it seems, were thought to identify too closely with Caliban, and so the white school commissioners feared for their daughters' purity and maybe for their own lives. With little awareness of the irony, the literalists were willing to sacrifice even the Bard, Dead White Male Number One, to protect Whiteness, entirely missing Shakespeare's essential anti-literalist lesson that in any *drama*, opposing characters *need each other* to establish their identity. Prospero and Miranda mean very little without Caliban. They rely on each other.

earn our consensus and then build structures for getting our agreed-on work done. The anti-communism of the 1940s and 1950s forced radicals to do some very deep thinking and organizing, leading to the great lurch forward of the 1960s. And though the style of the older thinkers may seem oblique or a little strained to us today, it was a pragmatic and productive response to not being able to come right out and say what they were thinking.

Of course, that has been the normal condition in America of black people in the presence of white power. Watching, waiting, encoding, finding and creating spaces for being fully human, and then, when possible, bursting into the open. The strategies in this book are not at all new. They are simply names for very old currents in the river of the black freedom struggle that Dr. Harding and many others have described. What is new is how each generation uses these strategies, how they play out in the specific context of the time. We can have a say in that, if we want, young or old, black or other. Each has a potential role to play, though it might take a good deal of rehearsing and practicing before we are able to play our roles persuasively.

What we can be sure of, though, is that one way or another, the next insurgency or lurch forward will be begun by a group of young people in poverty. Trying to understand what they are doing, trying to understand how they affect us and what stances we might try out in response and in support will always be time well spent. In this way, we try to encounter young people in schools of poverty as persons, rather than as things, the highest ethical demand we are able make on ourselves or on each other.

For Bob Moses, this issue is couched in constitutional terms. He describes the process of Africans in America moving from the status of constitutional property before the Civil War, to constitutional aliens from the end of Reconstruction to the 1960s. As long as education (the subtext of the Civil War constitutional amendments) remains implicated in the caste system of Jim Crow, neither Africans in America nor any other low-caste people will attain the status of "constitutional person." Chief Justice Taney's opinion in *Dred Scott* remains in effect:

> They [those "whose ancestors were imported into this country, and sold as slaves"] are not included, and were not intended to be included, under the word "citizens" in the Constitution, and can therefore claim none of the rights and privileges which that instrument provides for and secures to citizens of the United States. On the contrary, they were at that time considered as a subordinate and inferior class of beings, who had been subjugated by the dominant race, and, whether emancipated or not, yet remained subject to their authority, and had no rights or privileges but such as those who held the power and the Government might choose to grant them.

And Justice Taney also made clear in his opinion that "one of [those] rights is the privilege of suing in a court of the United States in the cases specified in the Constitution."

As far as education is concerned, "whether emancipated or not," descendants of slaves are still at the mercy of those who hold power, with no legal right of redress. As I write, an interesting manifestation of this inferiority is being played out, with dramatic irony, in Philadelphia, where the Constitution was written. Neither the City of Philadelphia nor the State of Pennsylvania can guarantee that the public schools will open this year, and if they do open, the students will be without any art, music, or extracurricular activities at all, because of budget shortfalls. This is not a sudden development, but has been growing for years, and not only in Philadelphia. *San Antonio vs. Rodriguez* established in 1973 that no student in any state has standing to sue in federal court to demand an education. The students of Philadelphia are at the mercy of the State of Pennsylvania just as much as the sharecroppers of Greenwood were at the mercy of the State of Mississippi when they went to register to vote. The solution to the voting rights problem could not be solved in Mississippi, but required the *country* to intervene. Appeals needed to be made to the federal courts and to Washington before federal marshals could be ordered to protect black people who wanted more than second-class electoral citizenship. But second-class *educational* citizenship is exactly what the descendants of slaves and other young people in poverty now have. When their schools fail to open, or when all their art and music classes are canceled, the students of Philadelphia do not enjoy the privilege of suing for educational justice in a court of the United States. So they must take matters into their own hands.

In fact this work has already begun. Young people of the Baltimore Algebra Project, the Philadelphia Student Union, Youth United for Change (also in Philadelphia), the Boston Youth Organizing Project, Project South in Atlanta, and Coleman Advocates in San Francisco, are appealing to the U.S. Attorney General and the President to intervene in Philadelphia in the name of the constitutional right to an education that is implicit in the 14th and 15th amendments. Again, this appeal or constitutional maneuver is *not* an end in itself. It is an organizing tool whose first audience is not government officials, but other young people who must learn how to develop a consensus and then structure an insurgency that will make the currently existing system of schooling impossible to maintain.

The students are using as their organizing vehicle a concept known as the National Student Bill of Rights for all Youth (NSBR), which would add enforceable rights to the U.S. Constitution as a way to extricate education from Jim Crow. Among these rights are not only topics narrowly referring to schools, but also the "arrangements," as Ella Baker calls them, without which young people cannot meet their educational needs. These are rights that are taken for granted in many other countries and by the upper classes everywhere: the right to transportation, to healthy food, to college access without economic barriers, to recreation, to housing, to employment, to security from warrantless detention, search, and seizure. And of course there are concretely educational rights: the right to study about one's own community and about the community's struggle against oppression; the right to study advanced mathematical and scientific topics with small enough classes and skilled enough teachers that the material can actually be mastered; the right to develop systems of peer teaching and other strategies that result in educational expertise arising indigenously from the community itself, rather than being imported; the right to use all kinds of art—music, drama, dance, visual arts, poetry, electronic media—to celebrate and expand the community's cultural traditions.

The National Student Bill of Rights has a long way to go before it enters the Constitution, but if the past is any measure, this battle is likely to be won in the end. The concept of who is a constitutional person has expanded over the centuries, and is likely to continue to expand until it includes young men and women descended from slaves. But it is still only a tool, a vehicle, for organizing. NSBR is an example of young people articulating their own interests, building consensus across first small and then larger geographic areas, and then devising ways and structures for advancing the aims they have decided are important. When the young people of Philadelphia, Boston, and Baltimore collaborate in this phase of the struggle for freedom, they are not doing anything new or unusual in the country's history. People from Philadelphia, Boston, and Baltimore have met before to secure the blessings of liberty for themselves and their posterity. Young people from SNCC and young immigrants more recently have talked, strategized, and acted for purposes that they agreed were important to the country in order to establish justice and to promote the general welfare. What would be somewhat new is for teachers and other adults to study ways of supporting this kind of work. Can we learn to help young people rehearse their roles as organizers in relative safety, figure out with their families how to keep them fed and housed while they take political risks and develop political consciousness, give them room and time to heal when things go badly, and encouragement to continue in the face of powerful opponents? And can we do all this while the young people study their math, while we help them read and write, while we celebrate their human impulse to learn and to create, and while they work out how to fashion all this insurgency for themselves?

Maybe yes, maybe no. But there is reason to be optimistic, because it has happened many times before. The achievement of a system of education freed from caste will not end history, of course. Another struggle will be bound to follow. It is certain, though, that any students, young or old, involved in the creation of that new system will learn much more than school could ever teach them.

Works Cited

Blumrosen, Alfred and Ruth Blumrosen. *Slave Nation: How Slavery United the Nation and Sparked the American Revolution.* Naperville, Illinois: Sourcebooks, 2005.

Bowles, Samuel and Herbert Gintis. *Schooling in Capitalist America.* New York: Basic Books, 1977.

Burke, Kenneth. *A Grammar of Motives.* Berkeley: University of California, 1969/1945.

———. *A Rhetoric of Motives.* Berkeley: University of California, 1969/1950.

———. *The Philosophy of Literary Form.* Berkeley: University of California, 1973/1941.

Crable, Bryan. *Ralph Ellison and Kenneth Burke: At the Roots of the Racial Divide.* Charlottesville and London: University of Virginia Press, 2012.

Darling-Hammond, Linda, Audrey Amrein-Beardsley, Edward H. Haertal, and Jesse Rothstein. "Getting Teacher Evaluation Right: A Background Paper for Policymakers." American Educational Research Association (2011). http://www.aera.net/Portals/38/docs/About_AERA/GettingTeacherEvaluationRightBackgroundPaper(1).pdf. Accessed March 20, 2014.

Dewey, John. *The Later Works* (Vol. 7). Carbondale: Southern Illinois University Press, 1984.

Ellison, Ralph. *Invisible Man.* New York: Vintage International, 1995/1952.

————. *Shadow and Act.* New York: Vintage Books, 1972 /1953.

Empson, William. *Some Versions of Pastoral.* New York: New Directions, 1974.

Franklin, John Hope and Loren Schweninger. *Runaway Slaves: Rebels on the Plantation.* New York, Oxford: Oxford University Press, 1999.

Freire, Paolo. *Pedagogy of the Oppressed.* New York: Herder and Herder, 1970.

Freyer, Roland G. and Paul Torelli. "An Empirical Analysis of 'Acting White.'" National Bureau of Economic Research Working Papers Series, May, 2005. http://www.nber.org/papers/w11334.pdf. Accessed March 20, 2014.

Harding, Vincent. *There Is A River: The Black Struggle for Freedom in America.* San Diego: Harcourt Brace, 1981.

Holt, John. *How Children Learn.* New York: Da Capo, 1995.

James, C. L. R., Grace Lee, Cornelius Castoriadis, and James Bracey. *Facing Reality.* Chicago: Charles H. Kerr, 2006.

Kardos, Susan. "Not Bread Alone: Clandestine Schooling and Resistance in the Warsaw Ghetto during the Holocaust." *Harvard Education Review*, Spring 2002, 33–66.

Lemann, Nicholas. *Redemption: The Last Battle of the Civil War.* New York: Farrar, Straus and Giroux, 2007.

Moses, Robert P., Mieko Kamii, Susan McAllister Swap, and Jeffrey Howard. "The Algebra Project: Organizing in the Spirit of Ella." *Harvard Educational Review*, 59/4 (November 1989), 422–444.

Moses, Robert P. "Constitutional Property v. Constitutional People." In *Quality Education As a Constitutional Right: Creating a Grassroots Movement to Transform Public Schools,* ed. by Theresa Perry et al. Boston: Beacon Press, 2010.

Moses, Robert P and Charles E. Cobb. *Radical Equations: Civil Rights from Mississippi to the Algebra Project.* Boston: Beacon Press, 2001.

Oakes, James. (1986). "The Political Significance of Slave Resistance." *History Workshop Journal*, 22 (October 1989), 89–107.

Organisation for Economic Co-operation and Development (OECD). *Programme for International Student Assessments*, 2009. http://www.oecd.org/pisa/pisaproducts /pisa2009keyfindings.htm.

Olmstead, Frederick Law. *A Journey to the Seaboard Slave States.* New York, 1863.

Orfield, G., & C. Lee, C. "Historic Reversals, Accelerating Resegregation, and the Need for New Integration Strategies," August 2007. http://civilrightsproject. ucla.edu/research/k-12-education/integration-and-diversity/historic-reversals-accelerating-resegregation -and-the-need-for-new-integration-strategies-1/orfield-historic-reversals-accelerating.pdf. Accessed March 20, 2014.

Payne, Charles. *I've Got the Light of Freedom: The Organizing Tradition and the Mississippi Freedom Struggle.* Berkeley: University of California Press, 2007.

Reagon, Bernice Johnson. *If You Don't Go, Don't Hinder Me: The African American Sacred Song Tradition.* Lincoln: University of Nebraska Press, 2001.

Waldstreicher, David. *Slavery's Constitution: From Revolution to Ratification.* New York: Hill and Wang, 2009.

Wimsatt, William Kurtz. *The Verbal Icon.* Lexington, KY: University of Kentucky, 1954.

JAY GILLEN has taught math and English in Baltimore City Public Schools since 1987. In 1994 he became founding teacher-director of The Stadium School, a community-run public school. Since 1995 he has worked to support young people in the Baltimore Algebra Project, a student-run collective that has employed over 1,000 young people earning a total of $2.5 million. His three older sons have all worked with the Algebra Project in various ways. Jay lives in Baltimore with his wife, Diane Kuthy, and their youngest son, Matteo.

Support **AK Press!**

AK Press is one of the world's largest and most productive anarchist publishing houses. We're entirely worker-run

& democratically managed. We operate without a corporate structure—no boss, no managers, no bullshit. We publish close to twenty books every year, and distribute thousands of other titles published by other like-minded independent presses from around the globe.

The Friends of AK program is a way that you can directly contribute to the continued existence of AK Press, and ensure that we're able to keep publishing great books just like this one! Friends pay $25 a month directly into our publishing account ($30 for Canada, $35 for international), and receive a copy of every book AK Press publishes for the duration of their membership! Friends also receive a discount on anything they order from our website or buy at a table: 50% on AK titles, and 20% on everything else. We've also added a new Friends of AK ebook program: $15 a month gets you an electronic copy of every book we publish for the duration of your membership. Combine it with a print subscription, too!

There's great stuff in the works—so sign up now to become a Friend of AK Press, and let the presses roll!

Won't you be our friend? Email friendsofak@akpress.org for more info, or visit the Friends of AK Press website: www.akpress.org/programs/friendsofak